Running Room's Book on

Family Fitness

by John Stanton & Don Zabloski

© 2013, Running Room Canada Inc.
First printed in 2013
Printed in Canada

This publication contains the opinions and ideas of its authors and is designed to provide useful information in regard to the subject matter covered. The author and the publisher are not engaged in health or other professional services in this publication. This publication is not intended to provide a basis for action in particular circumstances without consideration by a competent professional. The author and publisher expressly disclaim any responsibility for any liability loss or risk personal or otherwise, which is incurred as a consequence, directly or indirectly, of the use and application of any of the contents of this book.

Publisher: Running Room Publishing Inc.
9750 – 47 Ave.
Edmonton, AB T6E 5P3
Canada

www.runningroom.com

Running Room's Book on Family Fitness / by John Stanton and Don Zabloski

Includes Index.
ISBN 978-0-9739379-7-8

Cataloguing data available from Library and Archives Canada.

Substantive Editor: Lee Craig
Graphic Design: Harsh Deep Verma, Jenn Whyte

Contents

Preface

Families across North America are faced with two major challenges when it comes to health: childhood obesity and aging baby boomers. Health-care providers are over-burdened with the pressures placed on the medical system. Obesity rates and Type 2 diabetes are at an epidemic level in our children and grandchildren, something that was unheard of 20 years ago.

The reasons are simple—not enough exercise and poor nutritional choices. In addition, poorly thought out government cutbacks have seen the elimination of many physical activities. Many school physical activity programs have been cut or eliminated. Civic and provincial sports programs have been pushed back to a user-pay system, and many sports activities are now affordable for only the more affluent families. Compounding the problem is a proliferation of fast-food outlets with high-fat and high-sodium foods. We need a return of the family gathering, once per day, or at least once per week, to eat and talk as a unit.

The lives of parents and of their children are over-organized. Kids have organized play dates, classes and lessons, but lack the sheer joy of playing and the social interaction with their family members and with other children that comes with it. What better time to connect and encourage activity and personal choices than a family meal? We need to eat and go for walks as family units. Children, like their parents, are hooked online with their PDAs; their education, social interaction, entertainment and communication happens while sitting in a comfortable chair. We need a return to physical and social activity; it must start and be maintained by the family unit.

We need more education on healthy nutrition and physical activity and earlier detection and action on lifestyle health-related issues.

This book will provide you an intelligent plan to engage your family in lifelong healthy living.

I want to thank our team of Mike O'Dell, Harsh Deep Verma, Jenn Whyte, Lee Craig and Sherece Burma for their talents in reaching our goal with the book.

This book is dedicated to all families.

John Stanton

Introduction

This book is a handy guide and reference written for parents, kids and mentors. It is designed to be used daily and is filled with information and ideas to inspire you.

The book is a collaborative effort with Don Zabloski and myself, John Stanton. We are a couple of dads who have raised their own families. I have written books and coached over 800,000 people on walking and running. Don's career has been one of mentoring thousands of young people and their families through his professional advice and leadership. Together, in this book, we will share some innovative approaches to engaging families to be active in ways that are proven to be productive and fun.

Obesity rates in our youth are at an epidemic rate across the country. One-third of children, ages 5 to 17, are overweight or obese. Adults don't fare much better, with 18% of them overweight or obese. We all know the problem lies with inactivity and poor nutritional choices. We also know that kids, just like their parents, are hooked on technology. Their personal interaction with others, entertainment, education and intuitive needs can be done from the comfort of a chair, on a PDA device—unlike their parents who had to at least haul their backsides over to the local library. Today, thanks to technology, kids have access to the best libraries in the world on any subject, from wherever they choose to lounge. While this is terrific from an educational and informational basis, it has led to a lack of exercise that is reaching crisis levels.

Families face a barrage of challenges, including time management, competition at every level, economic challenges and peer pressure. Where kids once walked to school, they are now driven to school or bussed. Few come home at lunch.

Far too many children are using convenient fast food outlets as for their lunchtime dining. Computerization advancements and the urbanization of our communities bring dynamic and positive changes. But those changes, also bring unique challenges for families.

Kids, for the most part, have lost their sense of play. One of the culprits is technology, which has caused a host of inactivity issues and poor nutritional choices. Junk food is often more affordable than real, fresh food. Cars have become more affordable. Movies, television, entertainment and education come at us from a proliferation of multimedia sources. And very few of these innovations call us to any sort of physical activity.

Unstructured play has been replaced by highly organized and expensive kids' sports. While some of this is terrific for sport development, many sports are now well beyond the budgets of many families. The Canadian Medical Association identifies income level as the recurring theme that underpins most social determinants. Poverty places children in some parts of our communities at a real disadvantage for health outcomes. Running and walking, which are simple, affordable and relatively easy to deliver, can help. In this book, we will show you how to get your family started walking and running, and also give you other affordable and playful options to mobilize kids of all ages.

The family unit is at the heart of the solution. Mentoring and encouraging lifelong decisions about nutrition and exercise is clearly the answer to the obesity epidemic. We also know while some kids will outgrow obesity, the vast majority will be faced with a lifetime of health challenges. So the time for action, by all of us, is now.

Chapter 1
Getting Started

Action Plan

How do families set an active lifestyle plan to deal with exercise and nutrition?

To start with, the adults need to be mentors who coach their kids, grandkids, nieces, nephews and neighbours. Teach them how to chase a soccer ball, run, jump and play. Your teaching must be both motivating and personally active. Your own participation will encourage kids to keep moving.

Yes, an investment of your time and some money is required, but keeping kids active, in shape and busy also keeps them out of trouble. The key is to make physical activity an enjoyable, year-round endeavour. It is also important to

create family time for you and your kids to stay active together. It will be quality time you spend together communicating and having fun.

Families need to work on developing a culture of fitness. Don't just send your kids to school, to camp or to a coach. Work at developing a culture of being fit for life and doing fun stuff as a family unit. Encourage your kids to bring a buddy to some of your family activities. They will learn the importance of mind and body activities and learn important life skills while playing with a buddy.

Both you and your kids will soon discover that having fun exercising is way more enjoyable and requires less effort from you than if they are sitting around idle or, worse yet, fighting with one another. Kids also need to be encouraged to create fun activities on their own. In doing so they learn how to develop friendships and learn to interact with others in a positive manner.

Variety is fun. Teach kids to enjoy a variety of sports to show them how much fun exercise can be. Include team sports, individual sports, skilful sports like karate and gymnastics, and

swimming sports. Kids need to discover for themselves which sport is really special, so expose them to a broad variety of sports.

Include family time together, it can be a play in the backyard, a hike, berry picking or building a snowman. Find activities that work on kids' intellect as well as their physical well being.

Get kids involved in organizing each other into teams and working as a team. Sports can teach kids to stop whining and just carry on and compete against themselves. One of the key aspects of play is to give kids the message to compete—but to compete first against themselves to be better.

Have some incentive goals and rewards to acknowledge children's personal achievement. Avoid contradictory prizes like a soda, ice cream or a chocolate bar. A gold star, a coloured ribbon or a special pasta dinner can be the perfect incentives.

Starting anything worthwhile takes courage, but the rewards are great and well worth the effort.

BRING BACK PLAY

A drive through your neighbourhood will often present the image of empty playgrounds. Children need some unsupervised playtime, but our society has unfounded paranoia and an overprotective culture around our children's playtime—statistical reports show that our playgrounds today are safer than ever, both in design and from crime. A paved school parking lot makes for a great street hockey arena. Your own backyard should be the primary zone for kids to play. They can be slightly out of sight but still within reach.

Planning is essential. Set out a plan for after-school activities and play time that avoids computer games or the TV. Children and adolescents should have 60 minutes or more of physical activity daily. That time should include aerobic, muscle- strengthening and bone-strengthening activities.

AEROBIC ACTIVITIES

In these activities the athlete learns to rhythmically move their large muscle groups. Running, swimming, dancing, jumping and cycling are all great choices. None of these activities are too technical, and they all increase cardiorespiratory fitness. These activities should be designed with a progressive overload. In simple terms, increase activity duration by about 10% a week.

MUSCLE-STRENGTHENING ACTIVITIES

These are exercises and activities designed to make your muscles do more work than usual. They can be part of play by doing things like tug of war, climbing in a playground, climbing trees or lifting games. They can also be structured and guided such as lifting weights in a gym or working with resistance bands.

BONE-STRENGTHENING ACTIVITIES

Young bodies require a force on the bone to promote bone growth and strength. This goal is best produced by impact with the ground in a weight-bearing activity. Running, brisk walking, basketball, soccer, badminton and hopscotch are examples of bone-strengthening activities, which also include aerobic and muscle strengthening.

AGE IS A FACTOR IN PHYSICAL ACTIVITY

Children are naturally active in an intermittent way, called active play. Watch the young children at a recess break as they enjoy free play. They run, hop, skip and jump naturally. In doing so, they develop their movement patterns and skills. During this play, they naturally alternate periods of vigorous activity with brief periods of rest. Parents are sometime sceptical when as adults they return to running and are coached with a run or walk combination, yet as kids we all do it naturally.

Muscle strength naturally increases with this playful approach to activity. Kids don't need formal muscle-strengthening programs such as weight lifting. Regular activity in itself promotes a healthy body weight and body image for the child.

As children mature into adolescents, the pattern of physical activity will change. They can now play organized games or sports for sustained periods of time. They can also introduce the use of resistance bands, or body weight, for resistance training. The much-loved push-up, sit-ups, squats and pull-ups can all be done in moderation. These exercises work on the major muscle groups of the body, legs, hips, back, abdomen, chest, shoulders and arms. Adolescents can also do some vigorous activities, such as soccer, running, swimming, jumping, skipping rope and cycling.

Children, at the start, will fall into one of the three groups. They will either be inactive, active on a daily basis or exceed the daily guidelines.

For those not active, you need to slowly increase their activity in small ways and in ways they enjoy. A gentle, yet progressive increase will keep them highly motivated and injury free.

CORNER STONE OF SUCCESS

Achieving family fitness and wellness requires appropriate year-round quality activities or group of activities. Make every family member part of the planning, assessment and accountability of your plan. Work on the plan together to develop physical activities, nutritional choices and ways to keep things fun for everyone. Family stress levels will improve as well as each member's personal self-esteem. Keep everyone committed and involved.

FITTING IT ALL IN

Time is precious for everyone, but what is more precious than your family? Like everything of value, family fitness requires your time and your mentorship. We make time for the dentist, the doctor and the lawyer. Make that appointment in your calendar for one hour of family fitness per day. Your family's health and wellness is well worth 4% of your time.

Family Body Image

Body image is how one sees and feels about their body. Children with a positive body image will exude more confidence and will take better control of the care of their bodies. Parents need to foster the promotion of healthy body image with their children.

Tips for Parents

- Be a positive role model by having a positive attitude toward food and exercise.

- Make time for family gatherings, meals and conversations.

- Place more emphasis on abilities and skills, rather than appearances.

- Explain to your child his or her body will change throughout puberty.

- Discuss media marketing messages and images and the relation to reality.

- Avoid making negative comments about individuals' bodies.

- Tell your child it's okay to show emotions, such as sadness, irritation and annoyance.

- Discuss peer pressure in our communities to look a certain way.

- Teach your children to be proud of who they are.

- As a parent, you need to have confidence in your own body image.

Healthy Sleep Habits

Getting enough sleep on a regular basis affects the mental and physical health and overall quality of life of our children. The quality and timing of your child's sleep will have them performing better in school and at play. Children ages 5 to 10 years require at least 10 hours of sleep per night, while teens 10 to 17 years require 9 to 10 hours of sleep. Failing to get adequate sleep, children will become more irritable, hyperactive, inattentive and temperamental. Too little sleep can affect growth and the immune system of the child.

Parents need to help the child maintain consistent sleep schedules both during summer vacation and the school season.

Routines and schedules for sleep helps your child unwind from a busy day. Often if our children haven't exercised during the day they will have trouble sleeping at night. Try to keep the schedule as consistent as possible throughout the year.

Photo credit: Anissa Thompson

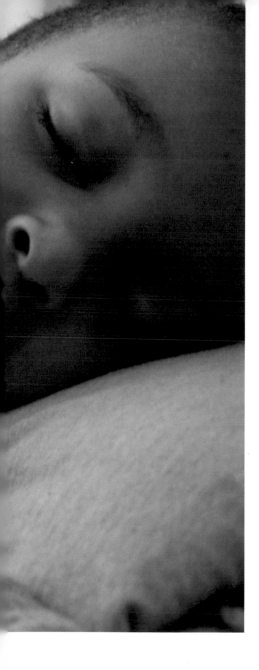

Here are some tips to help develop healthy family sleep habits

- A consistent time each evening

- A light healthy snack with a glass of milk or water, avoid sodas or iced tea with caffeine

- A warm bath

- Reading to your child has a calming and relaxing effect on both of you

- Keep the room quiet, dark and at a temperature comfortable for the child

- Unplug and remove television, video game, iPads, iPods and phones. Disconnecting them helps create a sleep-friendly environment

- Keep a sleep log to keep track of whether your child is getting adequate sleep

- Creating a calm, welcoming and relaxing atmosphere will help your child get a good night's sleep

Sleep is key to healthy living, allowing for recovery and renewal following periods of healthy stress.

Chapter 2

Our Active Living Plan

Our love of physical activity is visible. At the Olympics and Paralympics, people of all ages celebrated participation in physical activity. In 2010, the Winter Olympic Torch Run across Canada was wonderful, not only for the torch bearers, but for the many spectators as well. Communities came together to cheer and be inspired by the flame. The torch bearers included many everyday citizens and prominent community leaders who were recognized and rewarded for their past and present accomplishments.

When Canadian Olympic athletes are interviewed they often talk about their love of their sport. They also credit their extraordinary support system, which includes family, friends, coaches and their Canadian sporting associations. These athletes spend countless hours to train and compete, and, importantly, they have fun through it all.

This book's scope might be a little smaller, but the same thoughts and benefits for ourselves, family, friends, neighbours and community should be there. Parents and other family caregivers need to start or continue to shape the future physical activity and healthy eating habits of children. Changing behaviours and attitudes today will affect generations to come.

Renew, Inspire, Empower

Parents need to model positive behaviours and attitudes about healthy and active living choices for their children.

RENEW YOU

You have to help yourself before you can expect to help others. What will you do or are already doing to renew yourself? Are you healthy physically, spiritually, emotionally, mentally and intellectually? Perhaps you could partner up with someone—a spouse, another family member or a friend to support each other's renewal.

The Running Room knows of many personal stories and conversations that explain why people have joined Running Room training programs across Canada and the United States. People join to renew themselves physically and socially and to refresh their learning and understanding about a healthy lifestyle through walk or run programs.

INSPIRE YOUR FAMILY TEAM

Be a parent who is determined to inspire your family members to eat more healthily and be more active through positive messaging. Go out for your own walk or run and come back and tell everyone how great you feel. Take your family out with you the next time. Pack a healthy and tasty lunch that reflects *Canada's Food Guide.* You will have more energy through the day as a result. Create the opportunities for active family playtimes or bring everyone together for a weekly family meal. Your passion will soon be evident and visible.

EMPOWER YOUR COMMUNITY

Now that you have your home well on its way to being a healthy place and your family's healthy practices are visible, it's time to stir up the community.

Assist and volunteer with your children's school to demonstrate healthy school practices. We should see and hear students being active in a number of ways and times through their school day. Has a reverse lunch been considered—get out to play for 30 minutes before gathering for lunch? This way students are active after sitting for the last part of the morning, and more healthy lunches are actually eaten as a result. Can you share some healthy ideas for those special food days or assist to create a healthy nutrition policy that reflects the provincial or state guidelines? Have students been empowered to support a safe and caring environment, so that all students are mentally and socially fit and cared for?

Besides being at school for most of the day, what sections of the larger community are your children part of? Perhaps an organized sport or activity. Are all children playing and practising? Are the adult coaches positive role models? Do they explain their sport in the larger context of where it fits in terms of lifelong physical activity and age-appropriate development, both mentally and physically? Children enjoy playing with their friends. Is it a positive and friendly environment for all children? Do we see support from the spectators and positive cheering?

Many children love an organized sport. Support this activity and try to introduce a variety of other activities through family outings. The benefits of exposure to learning about and participating in a variety of physical activities over a lifetime, especially in a person's younger years, have been shown by research. Share with your children how all of these activities and sports are related and benefit each other.

Empower your workplace to be a model for others to emulate. Car pool, walking meetings and lunches, nutritious snacks for meetings, taking the stairs rather than the elevator and arranging lunchtime wellness classes will increase workplace productivity.

Empower your friends and neighbours to value health and make a healthy and active difference. This is another place children can come together during the day. Invite everyone to get out to play after school or work every day, before or after supper.

Enjoy your goals for renewing, inspiring and empowering yourself, those around you and your active and healthy family.

Exercise is a catalyst to awaken the spirit and give confidence in the family unit.

SMART Goals

Families are looking to have healthier, more active lifestyles. For those families who are at the beginning of a family wellness plan or for those who need a reminder, let's remember to guide ourselves with a few SMART goals. The intention is not to create more stress but to provide you with some direction to achieve your goals. SMART goals are fun, healthy lifestyle goals that enhance every family member's physical, social, emotional, intellectual and spiritual needs and aspirations.

SPECIFIC

Lifestyle goals need to be specific in that they clearly define the what, why and how of the changes you want to make. Instead of saying generally, "We want to be healthier as a family," say, "We plan to walk as a family at least one time during the week on Wednesdays after supper and one time during the weekend on Sunday afternoon. By the end of three months, we'll increase this amount to three times per week."

MEASURABLE

Your goals should be measurable, such as "We are going to walk for 30 minutes." As a result, you'll be able to manage them more easily. Your family members should be able to see changes occurring in themselves and other family members: "I can see that our family walks have brought us closer. We are talking more to each other, and we have picked up our pace and are walking farther over the last three months. Our pedometers are letting us know that we are getting closer to 10,000 steps per day."

ATTAINABLE

Goals should be attainable in that you should be able to figure out ways to make them come true. Your physical activity goals need to s-t-r-e-t-c-h you a little, so you and other family members can feel some success in doing them. It will take some commitment from everyone. An example, "We will walk together on Sunday afternoons." Or, "Let's increase the distance we walk by one block each time." Motivation results from the success everyone experiences at the end of each activity.

REALISTIC

A realistic goal is doable but not necessarily easy. Set the bar high enough for an achievement that is satisfying for all family members, such as doing an activity two times per week. For example, every family member will get the opportunity to plan and choose the walking route for each session.

TIMELY

Timely goals help you to set a target or an end time for what you want to achieve. There can be a short-term goal. For example, at the end of three months your family is going to walk together at least three times per week. Over a longer period, you can set a goal to walk as a family three times per week and also to be active as an individual an additional three times per week in activities of your choice.

School-Year Goals

School-aged children define what a family does in a year. From elementary to university, the family year begins and ends with each school year. The beginning of the school year is very hectic, but active families realize that they shouldn't have to make any major changes in activity and nutritional lifestyle goals. You just need to ensure that every family member is doing enough activity, 60 minutes per day, and eating healthy choices daily from the four food groups.

Family and individual goals can lead to numerous and important aspirations. You all have social, emotional, physical, intellectual and spiritual needs to aspire to. What aspirations will you be proud of over the next family school year? Below are a few goals that will bring inspiration to your lifestyle changes.

ROLE MODELLING

Role modelling by parents and other caregivers will continue to be an important influence for children of all ages. It is especially important for a teen's choices. Keep in mind that peer and other social media influences may affect your children's choices.

FAMILY ACTIVITY PACKS

Have age-appropriate backpacks for every family member. Encourage activity at school and work by including a proper fitting pack—no larger than a child's back—two wide padded shoulder straps equipped with both a waist and chest strap, and light in weight with several compartments for load distribution.

The contents for children include one or two things to play with, balls or other objects to catch or throw, rope to jump with, a piece of chalk to mark games with and also a few things to read. For moms and dads, include a pair of runners, clothing, an exercise mat, a dyna band and heart rate monitor or pedometer. Don't forget to share and invite others to play with you. Include a daily or weekly inspirational note in everyone's packs.

FUN ACTIVITY TIME

Value daily to weekly active time together. Share your backpack toys with each other. Parents play with your children. As they get older, you'll be glad you did.

ACTIVE TRANSPORTATION

Walk, run, cycle, skateboard or wheelchair

FAMILY MEALS TOGETHER

Value daily family meals together without the TV on. Focus on each other instead. Take turns planning and preparing menus, including choices from the four food groups, with a boost in fruits and veggies and protein alternatives. Make enough for the next day at school or work.

AFTER SCHOOL/WORK ACTIVITY

This is a valuable time of day for children. Encourage involvement at school or in community activities and programs. Access programs in your neighbourhood or school, so that "active transport methods" can get the children there quickly and safely. Parents can take turns supervising a "walking" school bus to the community recreation centre after school where both children and adult playtimes are provided.

BALANCE FREE PLAY AND ORGANIZED PLAY

Research supports the benefits of daily free creative playtime for all ages. It seems to be missing in many of our lives. Organized sports and activity programs are important as well for children, youth and adults to acquire the necessary skills to be confident and comfortable in those situations. Try not to have your children specialize in any one sport too soon. Participating in a variety of sports and activities throughout the year, especially at young ages—5 to 12 years—will better prepare them for the opportunity to specialize as necessary in their chosen sport or activity.

TEEN TIME—GET OUT OF MY WAY

Value the role modelling you have provided and get out of your children's way. Let them make their own activity and nutritional choices.

"under your own steam" to school or work, either the full way or part of the way.

PLAY WITH OTHERS

Value your play with each family member and invite others to play with you, especially those friends and colleagues that can benefit from your passion for daily activity. Great times to come together are at recess, lunch, during work breaks, after school, work or dinner and on weekends.

A FAMILY GYMNASIUM

Outdoors, outdoors, outdoors. Value playing outdoors all through the year in yards and on safe streets, green spaces, parks or schoolyards. Get out there with others and don't forget everyone's need to move on one's own for a private walk or run.

Healthy Choice Goals

Daily physical activity and healthy nutritional choices should be the "only" choices for every family member. These choices will provide everyone with the energy for completing their daily living routines. They also significantly contribute to everyone's emotional, social, physical and spiritual well-being. Daily physical activity plus daily healthy food choices equals enhanced mental health. It's never too late or too often to ask or remind ourselves as parents, caregivers or other significant adults, "What is the life we want for every member of our family?"

According to the 2004 Canadian Community Health Survey, one in four Canadian children is considered overweight Some children are fortunate to grow out of being overweight, but many don't. They can become adults with severe weight issues that can cause diabetes, heart disease and other chronic problems. The Heart and Stroke Foundation's 2013 Report on the Health of Canadians indicates that the final 10 years of many people's lives will be one of sickness and diminished capacity because of lifelong unhealthy lifestyle choices as children, youth, adults and seniors. Some of which may be caused by lack of daily physical activity and healthy nutritional choices.

To influence the necessary changes in the health system, responsibility must fall on individuals, families and communities to combat the growing number of overweight children, youth, adults and seniors. As active families you can collectively commit to a goal of demonstrating and encouraging daily physical activity and healthy nutritional choices and habits for all age groups. The health and wellness of all families in our community can be the goal. Let's be the most physical, healthy, nutritionally active families, neighbourhoods, communities, villages, towns, cities, provinces, states and nations in the world.

When setting goals, you are perhaps making a choice you've been delaying for some time. Each family member can make their own choices, or they can be collective ones or any combination.

Get up and go outside for a family walk-and-talk meeting to decide what is best or realistic for each family member and as a family. Your choices can be for the entire year or your initial choices may lead to other choices that can be addressed weekly, monthly or for other periods of time. Don't forget to share and bring along another family with yours.

GOAL Strategy Suggestions

Here are a few strategies to assist you in getting your family started:

- Include one more family activity playtime together during the week.
- Introduce one more new winter activity for the family.
- Include one more family meal together during the week.
- Get outside as a family on Saturdays and Sundays this year.
- Include one new fruit and vegetable in everyone's lunch bag each month.
- Take turns making family meals.
- Eat breakfast together.
- Sit less each day.
- Walk or run at a faster pace.
- Introduce a teen night where teens can play sport.

- Walk, run, cycle or swim at the local recreation centre once a week.
- Eat seven servings of fruits and vegetables each day.
- Include children's friends and their families for active outings.
- Celebrate birthdays at home and in the neighbourhood.
- Organize a community of families to walk, run, cycle or blade.
- Organize an all-teen girls' yoga nights— move from home to home.
- Create a weekly activity schedule for your children and their friends for after-school hours.

Family Days

Families that are looking to enhance their family's activity plan need to add variety into their schedules. The goal may be to try a new activity that all or one family member has desired for some time. Another goal would be to create a monthly family day, activity or carnival or festival day. Many Canadian provinces set aside provincial family days. They usually occur in February of each year. The intent is to highlight family activities and spending time together. Active families can establish such a day each month. For example, leave the car at home. You could get from place to place by walking, biking, roller blading or some other form of run- or walk-based activity. Each family member can pack a comfortable backpack with extra clothing and healthy snacks. Hop on a bus or LRT/subway to get to a park or recreation facility in your community.

During the winter months, take public transport to a local park or outdoor rink and go for a skate. Many communities have outdoor ponds or human-made lakes rather than a typical indoor rink. Make sure the lakes are open and safe for play. Signage should be present to allow for safe use. Pack your own skates or rent them.

Spend a day at a community fitness centre. Swim or play racket sports, volleyball or basketball or try the aerobic machines or take a drop-in class, such as yoga, Pilates or tai-chi. There are many cost-effective classes to choose from. Don't forget to take a dip in the hot tub, sauna or steam. Ah, now that's active living! When you return home have everyone pitch in to make a well-balanced supper that all have contributed to.

For your monthly family play days, give all family members a chance to contribute to the success of the day from a variety of activities, type of active transportation, to nutritious snacks for the day. This day doesn't have to be costly. Bring some play things—you'll be pleasantly surprised how creative you can be. You will move from being active in the winter to active in the summer.

Family Walks/Runs

The family that walks and runs together stays together. It's true. Families that are consistently active together usually stay together longer and come together more often in the future for those special runs or walks as family traditions.

You need to think about the desired outcome that you have in mind for your family's health. Share that outcome with your family. Doing so will help clarify and motivate each family member's understanding and commitment toward achieving the desired outcome. What do we want our family to look like and to feel like in terms of the benefits of the healthy lifestyle practices? What do we want them to learn? How will we experience success as a family?

The journey starts as early as possible with our children. Health-care providers encourage a healthy and active lifestyle for all moms-to-be. For children under two years, allow them to bend, kick, stretch and roll by themselves and with parents' assistance. Their first steps can be looked at as your first family walk and run together. An early start provides growing children with the knowledge and understanding that physical activity and healthy nutrition are normal practices for your family. Initially encouraged by their parents, children learn to make their own healthy choices and carry them into their futures.

When every family member has an opportunity to talk about and be engaged in the process, this sense of ownership prevails. Everyone feels like a partner in supporting and determining their family's wellness destination. Active and healthy children will naturally become active and healthy teens who will then become active and healthy adults and so on, into those senior years.

As parents, you can facilitate the process along the way. Set short-term goals and identify positive changes that have occurred as a family or with individual members. Sharing specific observations about changes since starting your family walk or run outings helps clarify that end picture of a healthy family. For example, everyone is able to walk or run three kilometres now after starting the first few sessions at one kilometre. You are also walking faster but at a comfortable pace for everyone. You're drinking more water as a family. Having every family member contribute in this way allows them to be the best that they can be. Taking the time to get out for those daily or weekly family walk or runs takes some work and planning by everyone involved.

Encourage and model daily activity for all family members. This may come from parents, one of the children who is most active, grandparents or family friends who are considered part of your family. Rather than taking the car, walk or run to school, work, stores, friend's homes or the library, anywhere that is reasonable. Be patient—the results will come. Remember, your goal is for a lifetime of active and healthy living. Performing daily routines under one's own steam will lead to a better introduction to those walk and run outings. Provide an opportunity for input about what the best time is that everyone can come together for a family walk or run.

Start with one family walk or run per week. During the holidays, when everyone is at home from school or work, add another one in. Have someone volunteer to make a schedule and stick it to the refrigerator door or entrance to your home. Don't discourage anyone from getting out on their own but save one special walk or run as a family.

Let everyone choose a variety of routes and distances through the neighbourhood. Routes around the block, schoolyards and walking paths can all be included. Create a neighbourhood walk/run map and post beside the schedule. Some days you can go in opposite directions around the chosen route. Consider getting on your bikes, riding a bus or hopping into your vehicle and going to a special place in your community for your walk or run—for example, a park or a trail system across town. To start, distances should be age appropriate for young children.

If you are just starting out as a family, consider progressing from slow walking to faster walking to a slow run over a series of outings. Everyone should be able to walk or run and carry on a conversation. Warm up with a two-minute walk, progress to a slow run for one minute, walk for a minute, slow run for a minute and then walk. For a cool down include some simple stretches at the end. The Running Room introductory walk/run schedule would be a great example to follow. Be patient—the results will come. Keep the distances and times appropriate for your family member's ages and levels of fitness.

Encourage everyone to stay together initially. As the outings continue, you'll start to notice some individual changes occurring in everyone's fitness levels. Some may be able to walk or run at a faster pace,

especially if they have been also getting out on their own. Recognizing and supporting those individual differences is important for everyone's motivation and self-esteem, but don't allow anyone to be by themselves. Have a buddy within your family. As the outings progress, ensure everyone starts together. If someone wants to go at a faster pace, allow him or her to go with a buddy, for an agreed upon period of time or distance and always in visual contact. Then everyone regroups and finishes the outing as a family just like you started.

Wear something special for the walk/run sessions. Is there an opportunity for any special walk/run shoes or an item of clothing to be purchased (e.g., wicking T-shirts, shorts. hats, jackets, socks).

Invite a friend, grandparent or other close friend to join you on some of the outings. You might meet at a special community park for a walk or run and picnic afterwards. Consider trying a variety of walk or run combinations—relays, intervals, rolling hills in a park, snowshoe walks—and on a variety of surfaces—sidewalk, grass, artificial track or in an indoor pool for water belt walking/running.

Plan to enter a family-oriented walk or run event, which are held at various times throughout the year. There are many worthwhile charity events that include a variety of age categories and distances for children, youth and adults or just stay together and walk or run the event together.

Goal setting for a lifestyle that includes many family walk or runs together will certainly lead to a lifetime of memorable and healthy family traditions that all family members can be proud of and benefit from.

Family Outdoor Playouts

Goal setting for family outdoor playouts through all seasons of the year may start with every family member writing down or shouting out their favourite outdoor activities or indoor activities that can be played outside. Consider any new activities that can be provided as realistically and economically as possible.

Next, Mom or Dad or one of your children can get a monthly calendar and think of the days and times that will actually work and make sense for the family. Be realistic. Saturdays or Sundays are usually good days and then perhaps one more day during the week to start. Write the activities on the calendar for the day and time that all family members can most likely come together. Perhaps on the other days, individual family members can write down their commitments to be active. This way everyone can get out for their own walk or run or participation in their own choice of activity.

Of course, we will have to post the calendar in a high-traffic area like the refrigerator or entrance to your home. By providing choices and writing down and posting our monthly fitness playouts as a family, we have made health and fitness a priority in our lifestyle plan. This may mean dropping something individually or as a family that is not as healthy to provide the time for our family outings (e.g., reduced screen time).

Next, a reminder to ourselves not to take on too much to start. Choose family activities that everyone can commit to and maintain for a great length of time. If you start too much too soon, you may end up losing a family member or stopping all together. As a family, everyone will experience success, feel good and have fun if the challenge is just right. Usually having fun and feeling good will motivate us to play it over and over again. Mom and dad, think of a day when you've been out for a walk or run or some other activity: a beautiful clear day, perfect temperature, the air smells great, your legs and arms are in auto drive, you are coasting along effortlessly, everything is working perfectly. We want all of our family members to have and experience these joys of movement.

Set your family up for success. We have a whole lifetime to plan goals for active living and healthy nutritional choices. Another consideration is to ensure that every family member schedules their family fitness appointments into their daily planners. Either hard copy or e-planners will work. By writing it down, we will look at this like any other important appointment. Let's keep it, not cancel it, because it makes us feel better as a family and we're energized to accomplish more together and as individuals.

If necessary, the next step in achieving our goal is to create an extended family community support system. Include your extended family of brothers and sisters, aunts, uncles, grandparents, close friends and neighbours out for a walk or run after supper. Perhaps this is a way that our non family social time can be enhanced by feeding off everyone's energy. Children are together. Boys, girls, and adults can carry on their meaningful conversations while being active.

Healthy and Active Daily Routines

Our goal for this year will be to make physical activity and healthy eating lifestyle choices for the whole family and build them into our daily routines.

Setting SMART goals for improving eating habits can be started by recording everything that everyone eats during one day. Compare the records to *Canada's Food Guide* at **www.healthcanada.ca**. It is the recognized Canadian standard for healthy, balanced eating patterns. The information is shared in many languages to include the dietary differences we see in other cultures and to provide all Canadians with direction for healthy and nutritious eating practices. Families can see where they practise good eating habits and where they may benefit from making some changes. Active families can set short-and long-term goals to improve in one small area at a time (e.g., include one more fruit and veggie to diets).

Strategy Suggestions

Here are a few healthy strategies or short-term goals:

- Help each other to complete a one-day food record.
- Talk about the value of continuous improvement in all areas of life.
- Set short- and long-term goals, e.g., eating most meals at home.
- Brainstorm ideas for healthy eating at home.
- Eat most meals at home.
- Eat at least one meal per day together as a family.
- Discuss what active children have eaten during the day, whether it is at school or a friend's home.
- Increase drinking water and reduce and eliminate sugary drinks, including pops, punches, cocktail juices, sports drinks.
- Grocery shop together as a family and discuss food choices.
- Research fast-food outlets and restaurants for nutritional information.
- Become more knowledgeable about nutrition food labelling.

Providing only healthy food choices is our ultimate goal. Everyone gets to choose from a variety of only healthy and nutritional food choices.

The Eating and Activity Tracker from the Dieticians of Canada is an excellent tool for families to use to track everyone's daily food and activity choices, get feedback on how you are doing and finding ways to help improve family choices (**www.dieticians.ca**).

The family Guide to Physical Activity for Children and Youth by Health Canada, suggests that we increase our children's physical activity every month until they are playing at least 90 minutes per day (150 minutes or more per week for adults). Many provinces in Canada have implemented physical activity initiatives in schools of 20 to 30 minutes of daily physical activity, so as families we can build from that to get to that doable 90 minutes per day for every family child and adult.

Raising healthy children requires investment goals for physical activity and healthy eating habits. Talk about your individual and family goals and accomplishments during family talk time or when performing other activities (e.g., a family driving trip). Sports programs are wonderful for those who enjoy the competition, so too are the free play activities of walking, running, cycling, skating, street or park games and hiking that can be included as a family.

ACTIVE IN YOUR COMMUNITY

Is there a playground, schoolyard or park close by? Can you go to a community centre, gym, pool or outdoor rink? Do you have backyards, nature trails, bike paths or side walks to play on?

You can use your collective map making skills to map how aware you are of the active play spaces in your neighbourhood. Choose a large piece of blank paper. As best as everyone can, draw in the streets, parks, schools, recreation centres and other play spaces that you are aware of. More can be added as you learn of them (e.g., tennis courts, rolling hills, sports fields). You can then label or put names to the sites and maybe add pictures, drawn or real photos. Then map out safe routes to get to each location. Next, create an active circuit or route on your map to get to each play space. For instance, you can walk, run or cycle along the active circuit to a spot, open space at a park, and exercise for a few minutes and then continue to another site, school tarmac, and perform another exercise. These may include sit ups, jumping jacks, hopscotch, four-square, yoga poses or stretches, hanging from the monkey bars and many more you can invent or recreate. Make your active circuit interesting by simply changing directions throughout your route. Okay, now that you have your neighbourhood play map and circuit, get out there with your family, friends and neighbours. It is a great way to meet and greet each other as new neighbours.

LEARN ABOUT JUMPING AND SKIPPING

February is Heart Health Awareness Month as supported by the Heart and Stroke Foundation of Canada and its many successful home and school programs and campaigns. One of which is the Jump Rope for Heart school program. You can support the jump rope school program because it raises millions of dollars for research and education to help keep Canadian children healthy. It reinforces community spirit and brings schools together for an active and worthy cause. It can also jumpstart your entire family into being more active and healthy at home. Here are some

jump activities to do at home starting in the month of February and continuing throughout the entire year.

First, do a walk or run warm-up for a few minutes and a few familiar stretches, especially for the legs. Have everyone in your family try jumping up and down on one foot/leg and then the other or on both feet on the spot. Try some jumping jacks with different arm movements. Think of some animals that jump, like a kangaroo, and have each family member form into a conga kangaroo line and jump around the play space. Are there other animals that jump? Try a musical jump dance routine with your favourite music.

To start, jump over a straight rope that is on the ground. Jump back and forth over the rope and start at one end and jump from side to side to the other end. Try doing a "limbo" under your rope. Have two family members hold each end of the rope and have everyone take turns going under, starting with the rope at head height and then slowly lowering it down. How about jump scotch? Place a rope on the ground and outline an area where you can throw an object, and then your children can jump on vacant spaces in the outlined area to get the object. Finally, have two family members hold each end of the rope. Then, have them just swing the rope back and forth so that everyone can try jumping over a moving rope. As you practise, your timing will improve. For more ideas and progressing to individual rope jumping, visit **www.heartandstroke.ca**.

CHOOSING HEALTHY FOODS

As parents you can provide a healthy food environment in your home by having "only" healthy food choices visible and easy to grab. Breakfast is a very important meal for everyone to become more productive in our daily routines at home, school, work or play. Try to sit down as a family to eat a daily meal as often as possible. Provide healthy foods and let your children decide on his or her portion size. Water from the tap or school fountain, milk choices and unsweetened fruit juices are excellent sources of liquids.

Active Thinking Skills for Everyone

One of the benefits of parents role modelling for their children is that eventually children will become active learners on their own. Children will consciously make decisions to go for a walk, run or play as they begin to internalize the benefits of daily physical activity. Here are a few fun and simple strategies to share with your children or any adult family member:

GOAL SETTING—Short-term positive goals that are achievable. For example, " Our goal for this playtime is to run with quiet feet. Today, we are going to run as quietly and softly as we can past two light standards and walk to the third one, and repeat the sequence for the whole route." Goal setting motivates children of all ages to monitor their growth and become self-reliant.

POSITIVE SELF-IMAGERY VISUALIZATION—Children, youths and adults see themselves as runners in their minds. Try to imagine the sounds of running. Listen to your feet. Can you hear your breathing? Can you see yourself crossing a finish line? Can you see your arms? Is your heart rate faster? Focus on different body parts as you run. Can you see, feel, hear, smell and taste the effects of running? Visualization enhances concentration on the key elements of a quality performance, like a video camera in your head that replays your running.

POSITIVE SELF TALK—This helps everyone, especially children, communicate their understanding of the running criteria. For example, keep your head up, be quiet on your feet, have your eyes forward, watch your foot placement—heel to toe or forefoot plant. "Come on, I can do this." Have your children self talk their way through a run by using short phrases or motivating words.

POSITIVE PICTURE WORDS OR PHRASES—These words are personally meaningful. They can add life to children's actions. For example, "I can run like my pet cat. My feet are like feathers touching the ground. I hold my hands like I'm carrying something I don't want to break apart." Active children may repeat these picture words a number of times throughout their walk or run. The words may assist children to remember what to do.

These active thinking skills may be used by themselves or in combination with each other. Express your picture word or phrase out loud to your running partner. Choose the most meaningful strategy that works for you.

Chapter 3

The Joys of Walking and Running as a Family

One sure way of getting everyone outside a lot more throughout the year is by planning and providing many opportunities for individual and family walks and runs. The idea is to enjoy walking and running as part of an active lifestyle for the rest of your life. Everyone can be successful and grow by learning to take ownership of their own walking and running choices.

How do we continue to make walking or running fun? Whatever the makeup of your family, role modelling by an active parent or caregiver is still the number one motivator for children and youth and other adult family members. As an adult caregiver, whether you are just starting out or are a seasoned walker or runner, walking and running are excellent strategies to bring your family together for your healthy family daily or weekly activities.

Try incorporating more movement into everyone's daily and weekly routines by including "active transport strategies": moving under your own steam to and from school, work or play situations. Walking, running, cycling, rolling to and from places that you frequent naturally become part of your family's lifestyle habits and behaviours. When you want to start getting out for longer walks or runs with your children the transition will be normal and successful.

Fun walks and runs should be viewed as playtime, or playouts, for all ages. Usually when people are playing, they are happy, smiling, laughing and enjoying their movements, whatever they may be, wherever they may be and

whatever they may bring. If moms and dads are having a fun walk or run, so will their children.

Try to walk or run in different directions. Look for natural changes that may be provided as a result of the various locations your walks or runs take you. Walking or running in straight lines can be reserved for later training or event situations. By varying your locations—neighbourhoods, parks, schoolyards, tracks, indoors or outdoors, open green spaces—you'll end up walking on various surfaces, including trails of various types, hills, perhaps a series of rolling hills of various sizes and grades, puddles to jump over or walk or run through or creative climbing playgrounds.

Adding to your enjoyment are the following: relays of all types, orienteering and scavenger hunts or GPS-type games in your community or across town; active picnics in your yard; special holiday walks or runs; attendance at and participation in community charity events; multiple events—tri events, with swimming, walking and running and biking; and walk- and run-based activities, such as skating, cross country skiing or going to watch a local road race event or school track and field. Children see other people walk or run, and that gives them secondary role models.

Invite another family member, another family or a friend of your children along for your walking or running playtime. Your children's friends or peers will provide much-needed and accepted motivation for their desire to walk or run as a

lifestyle choice. Walking and running as a family is great; walking and running with a friend makes children feel even more positive. After all, as parents or caregivers, we cherish those family walks or runs together, but we also look forward to the times when our children choose to walk and run on their own or with their friends as a result of your positive role modelling and healthy daily activity choices.

This sense of belonging—whether in a group, as a family team or team of friends—is very important for all ages. The Center for Advancing Health suggests that participation in walks or runs by female teens is especially influenced by their peers and friends. Their social and emotional needs can also be enhanced as can their physical needs. Walks and runs are completed together. No one gets left behind. You will soon find everyone's conversation pace. For those that require a little extra, they can continue on their own after their family or friends walk or run is completed. Perhaps start and finish with fun warm-up and cool-down challenges. Warm up with juggling activities of light scarves or other colourful objects or include a variety of yoga poses or stretches for a cool-down.

Everyone's motivation may be enhanced by special items of clothing, walking and running shoes, water bottles and the use of pedometers or heart rate monitors. Feeling and looking great while enjoying your walks or runs increases motivation.

Experiencing success early and often by including a few simple and, of course, fun goals will also encourage lifelong walking and running. Maintaining even pacing, increasing our distance by one block each week, finishing together, using our pedometers and having natural obstacle courses or changing three different routes to six different routes when you change the directions helps. Sincere praise with high-fives should be very specific in nature. Tell children what they were great at, whether it is their pacing, attitude, smiles, use of their sports watch or how they create a fun and challenging route for the family.

Initially, young children will develop a sense of ownership for walking or running by the many opportunities to play on their own, with mom or dad, other siblings or family members and with friends. Make a pre-schooler's walks and runs interesting by including many natural, creative and personal changes in direction, stops and starts and puddle jumps. Have a sit-down when the child is tired. You will never know where children might take you. Your responsibility is to keep the route safe and personal for those involved. In this way, your children are already being included in the decision-making for your family choices. As every year passes, they will become a little more aware and understand their involvement in family choices for walking and running. They will naturally accept daily and weekly decisions for how they get to routine activities and places or to special events. Being involved in active playtimes helps children with their interest in participating in other walk- or run-based activities and sports, e.g., soccer, hockey, lacrosse, wall and outdoor climbing, gymnastics or dance. They are so many sports and activities to choose from.

Family Fun Walking and Running Playouts

Walking and running for family fitness are inclusive activities that many children and youth can enjoy because they are convenient, inexpensive, enjoyable and healthy. They can be continued over a lifetime as a choice with many health benefits. However, it can be challenging to convince children and youth that walking and running aren't boring. The answer is to provide a wide variety of fun and challenging walking and running experiences.

With very young walkers or runners, have each child hold one end of a rope or scarf to keep family buddies together. Use written instructions for hearing-impaired children and youth. Arrange for a buddy family system for those children or youth in a wheelchair, alternating between wheeling themselves for short distances and being pushed. Slow the pace and provide rest periods.

Create an individual or family walking and running e-journal to record meaningful information, including goals: number of steps per day/week; a variety of safe routes and distances; neighbourhood map of routes; experiences and feelings during and after walks or runs; and key criteria for walking and running technique—head up, eyes forward, walk or run tall, back straight, shoulders relaxed and forward, swing arms opposite to legs, right arm and left leg forward, heel-to-toe contact with the walking surface.

A pedometer—step counter—can be used as a motivating tool by all ages, e.g., 10,000 steps per day for adults and 15,000 steps per day for children and youth.

Walking or Running Play Games

Organize your family and invite friends or other families into teams, whether two, three, four members, etc. Choose a variety of routes. Have the teams walk or run together and keep track of the number of laps or outings they complete in a certain time period, e.g., laps/outings per week as a team; distance; total steps per lap/outing per day/week/month/year. Have everyone record the information in their e-journals. Your team could discuss how you can motivate yourself to walk or run more steps and to complete more laps or outings. Are you enjoying your laps or outings? How can we make them more fun? What did you learn about your team members when you were walking and running and talking? Talk about the five things that were most interesting.

ALPHABET WORD GAMES

Organize into family teams that may include other families and friends. You will need one pen or pencil, one sheet of paper or an electronic pad of some type. Make up a simple alphabet or word play sheet that lists each letter of the alphabet. Explain that they will need to see and record at least one "thing" on their walking or running route that starts with each letter of the alphabet. Try to find and see as many letters of the alphabet as possible during their walks or runs over however many walking sessions. Emphasize the correct spelling of words. Once teams have finished, the lists can be shared. Challenges can be made by others to ensure these "things" were actually seen on their routes, e.g., where they saw it or take a walk to where the "thing" is located. The alphabet sheet can be included in their e-journal. This is an excellent game for getting to know your immediate neighbourhood or community. Learn about locations of the parks, schoolyards, open spaces, homes, buildings, trails and bodies of water in and around your place of residence.

WALKING AND RUNNING CALENDAR

To be included in your e-journal or posted on the refrigerator door or family message board: all family members can brainstorm to include a variety of individual or family weekly walking or running challenges on the calendar. Each family member can choose a minimum of three walking or running activities to complete in a week. Once completed, they can initial or check off that activity and write and talk about their thoughts about the activities and suggest any changes or improvements for next month. Some examples for activities: walk or run to a friend's home to talk with rather than phoning, texting or chatting by computer; walking or running your family or another family's pet; walking or running to and from school; walk or run up and down a neighbourhood hill; take a walk or run in a park, schoolyard or trail; walk or run a set of stairs; walk or run with a friend; walk or run at lunch; walk or run on the spot while watching a favourite TV show or walk/run during commercials; park in the farthest parking space from the shopping mall and walk or run to the mall; walk or run for one hour or a number of health benefits steps.

CREATING A SAFE WALKING OR RUNNING ROUTE

Have each family member create a safe and challenging walking or running route for family or friends to enjoy. Have them go out for a walk or run with their friend or family member to create and record a very specific route. As parents, we may want to designate the immediate neighbourhood with boundaries within which the routes can be created. These boundaries can vary with age. After they return, they can talk about the route and its challenges or how to make the route more interesting. Maybe ask for a parent's advice and assistance and approval. Usually, children's walking or running routes will be more interesting and fun than just a walk or run around the block.

HEART RATE WALK OR RUN

Have each family member take their pulse prior to, during and after the walk or run As a reminder, you can take your pulse on the carotid artery or the wrist for the best and most consistent locations. Count the beats for six seconds, and then multiply by 10 for your heart rate per minute. Walking or running activities can show that different intensities of exercise have different effects on your heart rate and in normal and healthy situations are okay:

1. walk or run slowly around a specified play area for one minute; take your heart rate

2. walk or run as fast as you can for one minute in the play area; take your heart rate

3. rest for two minutes; take your heart rate

4. walk or run on a flight of stairs at home or a rolling hill in a park for one minute; record your heart rate

5. your heart rate can be taken and recorded as you are walking or running

CHANGE OF PACE

Changing your pace on some of your walks or runs and determining your heart rate can provide needed motivation. For teens and youth or for adult family members, awareness of their target heart rate zone may also be a motivating factor to improve their cardiovascular endurance. This may be the time to look at sport watches and heart rate monitors for family use.

LOOK AT YOUR PACING

Have your family members estimate the time it might take them to complete one of their chosen routes prior to going out or the number of steps that might be recorded on their pedometer (should be a specific distance, such as one or two kilometres). Record everyone's estimates. When everyone returns, record their actual times or steps or both. Enjoy a conversation about everyone's actual and estimate numbers.

PLAY THE PASSING GAME

Organize your family members and friends into a straight line of four to eight people. The first person in each line carries an object, e.g., soft stuffed animal, large coloured ball. As the team walks or runs forward, the first person hands back the object to the person behind him or her The game continues until it reaches the last person in the line. Then, they walk or run forward at a fast pace to the front of the line and the sequence is repeated. This can be repeated for a specific time or distance. You can start the object with the last person passing forward to the front, then the person steps to the side and walks or runs backward or waits stepping in place until the line passes them and they join in at the end of the line.

TOUR DE NEIGHBOURHOOD

The most active walking or running family member gets to wear the "yellow jersey" to recognize their commitment to walking or running or another worthy goal accomplishment. The item of clothing should be passed around between each family member to recognize everyone's accomplishments and yet continue to keep the jersey a special motivation.

CATCH YOUR BUDDY

Designate a track-like area at your local schoolyard, e.g., around a sports field or use a track if present. Start at opposite ends/sides of the track. One person will walk or run at their normal pace and the other will walk or run as fast as they can to catch their buddy. Once they are caught, then the roles are reversed and they start again. Parents can make this activity more challenging by having walkers or runners reverse directions and roles on a signal, e.g., voice switch; use of a whistle. The challenge can also include both walkers or runners, walking or running at their own fast pace, trying to catch their buddy with parents calling or whistling switches for direction.

FAMILY RELAYS

Family members with friends can be organized into relay teams. Each team member walks or runs a certain distance (keep it short), returns, gives their teammate a high-five and then the next person walks or runs out on the course. The course distances should be 25, 50, 100 or more metres to start progressing in distance as requested. When someone returns have them take their heart rate. Once everyone on the relay team completes one try, repeat a second time in the reverse direction. The relay can also be completed as a continuous relay. Place your teammates at various locations around the track. Two teammates need to be at the start point. One of them will start the walk or run to the second person. The first person stays at their spot, and the second person walks or runs to the third person. The sequence continues until everyone returns back to the spot on the track or course they started at.

ORIENTEERING/SCAVENGER/ TREASURE HUNT

Send your family and friends out on a walking or running scavenger/treasure hunt. Equip them with a properly fitting backpack and a list of items to collect, such as a signature from a neighbour, a white rock, a piece of coloured paper, a fallen leaf, a business card from a local business, a fallen twig or a discarded beverage container. You pick up as many discarded or naturally fallen things as you can in 30 minutes. Parents may also hide controls/clues (sheet of paper with a clue written on it) along a favourite and safe walking route and have family members try to find them. On the controls/clues a special question can be included for the finder to answer. Some questions may include, name the four food groups; name a famous person in your city; or name two places on your body that you can take your heart rate or pulse. Be creative with your questions. How about school homework review questions? Have each family member create different questions and their own routes for others to follow. Take your family to an orienteering event in your community. Also, check for any recent geo-caching GPS opportunities in your community. They are very popular for all ages as well.

TAKE ALONG SOMETHING TO PLAY WITH

On your walk or run, take a skipping rope, exercise dyna band or a variety of balls to play with. Every so often, stop and jump rope, stretch with your exercise band or pass a ball around in an open play space for a few minutes and then continue your walk or run. Repeat every 1,000 steps or five-minute period walks or runs.

MAP READING

Have your active children draw or make use of an e-map of their own backyard, nearby park or open green space with trails. Map out a variety of routes. For a hardcopy map, use a coloured marker, and draw a path on each map. You may want to laminate or cover the maps with plastic wrap for protection against the elements and sweaty hands. Go out as a family or in buddy pairs for safety. Review the maps with your children, and then away you go. If several maps are made, various family groups could walk or run different routes and switch maps for each outing. You may consider making a map with landmarks and no designated route outlined or a map with the route marked and your children can fill in the landmarks. An alternative would be to give each team a coded map with lines indicating different movements. For example, a straight line for walking or running, a broken line for skipping and a wavy line for galloping or just write the movement at different locations on the map. Name the different areas on the map with animal names. As the teams go through that area, they must move like the animal that lives there. You might even set up stations at various locations where everyone could perform an exercise, such as five jumping jacks, six tuck jumps and four one-legged hops on each leg.

There's no limit to ideas and challenges for families to have fun-filled activities incorporated into their walks and runs. Keep trying to motivate your children and other family members or friends to be active and involve them in wonderful creative walking and running ideas and challenges. They will appreciate your efforts in guiding them toward a healthy active lifestyle.

Let's Go for a Walk or Run

Walking and running are convenient, inexpensive, lifelong, healthy activities that are inclusive for millions of people and families worldwide. Here is a simple "let's go for a walk or run" plan that parents and other caregivers may consider for their family, friends and soon-to-be neighbourhood friends.

To receive the maximum benefits of these walks and runs, families should consider going out together for at least three playouts per week with one or two rest days in between.

Pacing and not racing are good reminders for everyone starting out, especially for children. Pace yourselves with the talk test. If you are having difficulty carrying on a conversation, then you are walking or running too fast. Initially, it is important to stay together for your family walks and runs.

If one or more family members is just starting out, consider a family walk program together for a number of weeks and progress to a run program as necessary. Walking together or running together should be gentle and have progressive strategies. Walking breaks during the Running Room run programs have proven to be a very positive strategy for many adult runners.

The use of a pedometer as a step counter is a useful tool to enjoy your family walks. Your goal will be to progress to 10,000 steps per day for adults and 15,000 steps for children and youth—adjusted for step length and benefits. As well, families can introduce themselves to the use of a heart rate monitor during their walks or runs as another useful tool for everyone's interest and motivation. Everyone enjoys a little technology in their lives. Pedometer prices vary, but they are usually very economical as a family purchase or one for the family to share on each outing. Heart rate monitors also vary in price depending upon the variety of options chosen. Neither tools are necessary, but they may be considerations as everyone's progress advances. The important thing is to just get out there for many walks and runs as a family. Information on these tools can be sourced from the Running Room resource centre at **www.runningroom.com**.

Sample family talks may include the following: walking and running form, although anything goes for your young children; understanding the benefits of walking and running or why it's good for your legs, arms, breathing, brain and heart and for participation in other activities and sports; target heart rate zone—for children, hand on my heart and why is it beating faster, where else can I feel my pulse beat on my body; we're walking and running like what animals?; family meetings while walking and running; practising your pacing or how fast will you walk and or run; I'm thirsty—what can we get to drink before, during and after the runs and walks?; I'm hungry—what can we eat before, during or after our walks or runs and what is best?; how far can we go? Can we count our steps? Where are we going to walk or run; and can we bring our friends? There are many more topics or information on the Running Room website (**www.runningroom.com**).

Let's Go for a Family Walk

This family play walk is for those just starting out as new active walkers and for those establishing a regular and consistent family walk routine. Please refer to *Walking—A Complete Guide to Walking Fitness, Health and Weight Loss*, by John Stanton, for many more ideas, information and plans that will make your family walks enjoyable, challenging and progressive for all family members. Enjoy your family walks together for a lifetime.

WEEK 1

Family discussion: Why are we walking? (three to five minutes during our juggling warm-up or during our walk)
Go for a walk. Route #1: 15 minutes done three times during the first week.

WEEK 2

Family discussion: Safe walking routes and tips (three to five minutes during our quiet and soft marching-on-the-spot warm-up or during our walk)
Go for a walk. Route #1: in reverse—20 minutes done three times during the second week.

WEEK 3

Family discussion: Walking form—head and shoulders, knees and toes (three to five minutes during our yoga breathing exercises or during our walk)

Go for a walk. Route #2: 25 minutes done three times during the third week.

WEEK 4

Family discussion: What do we get to wear? Safe and functional clothing (three to five minutes during our family dance step musical warm-up or during our walk)

Go for a walk. Route #2: in reverse—25 minutes done three times during the fourth week.

WEEK 5

Family discussion: What do we get to drink and eat? (three to five minutes during our group crunch, plank and water sip warm-up or during our walk)

Go for a walk. Route #3: 30 minutes done three times during the fifth week.

WEEK 6

Family discussion: Happy hearts—walking is good for your heart. Heart rate monitors? (three to five minutes during our dyna bands warm-up or during our walk, and bring along the dyna bands and take turns with the heart rate monitor or simply take your pulse every so often during the walk)

Go for a walk. Route #3: in reverse—35 minutes done three times during the sixth week.

WEEK 7

Family discussion: Lots of questions? (three to five minutes during our rope skipping warm-up or during our walk. Bring along the skipping ropes to use along the way)

Go for a walk. Route #4: 40 minutes done three times during the seventh week.

WEEK 8

Family discussion: We are going to walk like…what animal? (walk like an animal, speed walking, race walking, poles, different types of play walking)

Go for a walk. Route #4: in reverse—45 minutes done three times during the eighth week.

WEEK 9

Family discussion: We're feeling great! What are the social and emotional benefits? (three to five minutes during our we-get-to-laugh warm-up. Take turns telling a joke that makes everyone laugh during your walk)

Go for a walk. Route #1: 50 minutes done three times during the ninth week.

WEEK 10

Family discussion: Counting our steps. Use a pedometer. (three to five minutes during our let's-set-up-our-pedometers-for-us-to-use warm-up)

Go for a walk using the pedometers to see how many steps you take. Can anyone guess the number of steps? Route #1: in reverse—55 minutes done three times during week 10. How many steps did each person take individually and then as a family? What's the total for the week?

WEEK 11

Family discussion: Walking up and down hills like you are little kids again! (three to five minutes during the anything-goes warm-up or during the walk)

Go for a walk with the pedometers to a park, schoolyard or open space with rolling hills. How many steps did each of you take going up each hill and did you take the same number of steps going down each hill? Sixty minutes done three times during week 11.

WEEK 12

Family discussion: Activity choice—partner relays, catch-and-tag your partner, conga line walk. (three to five minutes for a warm-up)

Go for a walk. Let's take 8,000 to 10,000 steps today—10,000 steps per day, you bet!

Let's Go for a Family Run

This family fitness/play run is for those just starting out as new active runners and for those who are establishing a regular and consistent family run routine. Please refer to *Running: The Complete Guide to Building Your Running Program*, by John Stanton, for many more ideas, information and and plans that can be adapted for your family runs. Enjoy your family runs together for a lifetime of family traditions.

NOTE: This run is for children ages eight years and older who have been active with their families for at least 60 minutes per day most days of the week or are participating in community sport (e.g., hockey, soccer) or activity (e.g., dance, gymnastics) programs. This sample has been adapted from *Running: The Complete Guide to Building Your Running Program*, by John Stanton, pp. 128–29. Please refer to p. 130 for the intermediate running program—three family walk and run playouts per week with one or two rest days in between each playout day.

WEEK 1

Family discussion: Why are we running together? (three to five minutes during our juggling warm-up)

Go for a walk/run. Route #1:

1. walk 1 min.; run 1 min.; walk 2 min. x 6 sets
2. followed by run 1 min.; walk 1 min.
3. Total time—Running 7 min. Walking 14 min.

WEEK 2

Family discussion: Safe running routes and tips (three to five minutes during our quiet and soft marching on the spot warm-up)

Go for a walk/run. Route # 1: in reverse.

1. walk 1 min.; run 1 min.; walk 1 min. x 10 sets
2. Total time: Running 10 min. Walking 11 min.

WEEK 3

Family discussion: Running form (head, shoulders, knees and toes) (three to five minutes during our yoga breathing and pose exercises)

Go for a walk/run: Route #2:

1. walk 1 min.; run 2 min.; walk 1 min. x 6 sets
2. run 2 min.; walk 1 min.
3. Total time: Running 14 min. Walking 8 min.

WEEK 4

Family discussion: What do we get to wear? Safe and functional clothing and footwear. (three to five minutes during our family dance step musical warm-up)

Go for a walk/run. Route #2: in reverse.

1. walk 1 min.; run 3 min.; walk 1 min. x 5 sets
2. Total time: Running 15 min. Walking 6 min.

WEEK 5

Family discussion: What do we get to eat and drink? (three to five minutes during our group crunch, plank, and water sip warm-up)

Go for a walk/run: Route #3

1. walk 1 min.; run 4 min.; walk 1 min. x 4 sets
2. Total time: Running 16 min. Walking 5 min.

WEEK 6

Family discussion: Happy hearts—walking and running are great for your heart. Should you use heart rate monitors? (three to five minutes during our dyna band warm-up. Share a heart rate monitor with every family member or simply take your pulse every walking break)

Go for a walk or run. Route #3: in reverse.

1. walk 1 min.; run 5 min.; walk 1 min. x 3 sets
2. run 2 min.; walk 1 min.
3. Total time: Running 17 min. Walking 5 min.

WEEK 7

Family discussion: Lots of questions? (three to five minutes during our rope skipping warm-up)

Go for a walk or run: Route #4:

1. walk 1 min.; run 6 min.; walk 1 min. x 3 sets
2. Total time: Running 18 min. Walking 4 min.

WEEK 8

Family discussion: We're feeling great! Running and walking has social and emotional benefits (three to five minutes during our laughing warm-up. Everyone gets to share a joke that makes us laugh)

Go for a walk or run: Route # 4: in reverse.

1. walk 1 min.; run 8 min.; walk 1 min. x 2 sets
2. run 2 min.; walk 1 min.
3. Total time: Running 18 min. Walking 4 min.

WEEK 9

Family discussion: walking/running for a lifetime (three to five minutes during our-anything-goes warm-up)

Go for a walk or run: Route #1:

1. walk 1 min.; run 10 min.; walk 1 min. x 2 sets
2. Total time: Running 20 min. Walking 3 min.

WEEK 10

Family discussion: High-five week—what's next? A community charity event? Yahoo! We did it together! (three to five minutes during our everyone-leads-a-stretch warm-up)

Go for a walk or run: Route # 1: in reverse.

1. walk 1 min.; run 10 min.; walk 1 min. x 2 sets
2. Total time: Running 20 min. Walking 3 min.

Warm-up Activities— "Get Your Heart Pumping"

Prior to going out for a family walk or run, do a family warm-up. The length of the warm-up may vary from 30 seconds to five minutes depending on your family's age, fitness level, variety of warm-up activities and distance to walk or run. Prepare everyone both physically and mentally for more vigorous activity by doing the following:

Gradually elevate your heart rate (HR) with a few simple aerobic activities. Keep activities simple by moving major joints (neck, shoulder, trunk, hips, knees and ankles) through their normal range of motion. Remember to avoid deep stretching until muscles are warm.

Every few minutes through the warm-up and walk or run, have everyone take their HR by placing two fingers at the side of their neck (carotid artery) and take a 10-second count. Just a simple indication of increased HR under normal activity situations is a good thing.

Warm-up challenges may include

- walk or run slowly in a designated play area
- free faster walking or running and dodging with lots of turns
- skipping, galloping, side-steps and crossovers
- walk or run slowly forward, sideways, backward and shuffle steps
- walk or run slowly along the sides of your yard and walk or run quickly on the ends
- walk or run slowly along the ends of your yard and walk and or run quickly along the diagonals
- shadow walk or run with switches; partner walk and or run; follow the leader; shadow your partner. Encourage the leader to create many interesting patterns. Switch the leaders every 20 to 30 seconds
- relays—distances may vary but start with short distances to walk or run

Keep the challenges fun. Everyone contributes their walk or run ideas. Family warm-ups include smiles, excitement, high-fives and maybe everyone's favourite music.

Active Stretching

After the easy aerobic activities include a few active stretches to increase mobility while still keeping the HR elevated. Active stretching exercises increase muscle flexibility and the range of motion at the joints. For walking and running, stretch the large muscle groups and those muscles to be used while walking or running. The phrase "head to toe" stretches may assist with remembering the order.

NECK STRETCHES

1. slowly bend neck to the left side (left ear to left shoulder). Hold for 5 to 10 seconds

2. repeat to the right side

3. slowly bend neck forward (chin to chest). Hold for 5 to 10 seconds

4. slowly roll head back and forth across chest from shoulder to shoulder in a half circle; repeat 6 times

REACH AND STRETCH

1. clasp hands and stretch arms overhead; hold for 5 to 10 seconds

2. pull arms backward gently and hold

ARM CIRCLES

1. slowly circle arms forward for 5 to 10 seconds

2. slowly circle arms backward for 5 to 10 seconds

3. circle with arms straight, bent or elbows leading

SIDE LUNGES

1. stand with feet shoulder-width apart, and knees slightly bent, hands on the hips

2. move slowly from side to side by alternating bending and stretching each leg

3. hold stretch at each side for 5 to 10 seconds

SHIN STRETCHES

1. stand with feet shoulder-width apart

2. lift one foot and move it behind the other; gently press the top of the toes into the ground

3. knee of other leg is slightly bent

FRONT LUNGES

1. place one leg straight behind you, and the other leg in front with the knee bent at 90 degrees; feet are spread shoulder-width apart

2. hands are resting on the front thigh or on the ground beside the feet

3. hold for 5 to 10 seconds

4. switch the front/back legs, and repeat

SHOULDER SHRUG AND ROLL

1. shrug both shoulders upwards to ears and hold for 5 to 10 seconds; repeat five times

2. arms at sides, slowly roll shoulders forward in a circular motion; repeat five times

3. repeat, rolling shoulders backwards five times

4. repeat, alternating each shoulder forwards five times

5. repeat, alternating each shoulder backwards five times

HIPS AND WAIST

1. twister—knees slightly bent with feet shoulder-width apart

2. keep the hips forward, and slowly twist the upper body from the waist up, twist to look behind—hold for 5 to 10 seconds

3. repeat to right and left sides

KNEE TO CHEST

1. can be performed while standing or laying on one's back

2. lie on back with legs bent and both feet flat on ground

3. hold onto one leg and gently pull that bent leg toward the chest;hold for 5 to 10 seconds

4. slowly straighten leg

5. repeat with other leg

6. repeat 2 or 3 times with each leg

There are many more stretching techniques, but these should get you started. Keep it simple and fun. The total duration of aerobic and stretching activities may be from 5 to 10 minutes.

Use a variety of movement patterns to enhance a combination of walking and running activities:

- walk or run in a figure eight; vary the size of your eights
- walk/run to form a rectangle, square, triangle or other familiar shapes of various sizes; run the lengths and walk the sides
- walk the widths and run the diagonals
- partners or groups; the lead walker or runner leads the group to wind into concentric circles. When leaders reach the centre, they rewind the group out of the concentric circle
- have partners or groups form an inner and an outer circle. Have the inner circle walk or run clockwise, and the outer circle counter clockwise. On the count of three, both groups start running in their circle and every time they pass each other they give either a high- or low-five with that person

- outdoor circuits/stations—set up several stations in a variety of locations in a schoolyard, park or sports field. Vary the distances between the stations. Have everyone walk or run between the stations and complete the exercise at each station, e.g., jumping jacks, curl-ups, push-ups, rope skipping
- invite another family and friends along to try a file run. The team walks or runs in single files, behind each other with 2 to 3 metres between each person. Encourage the leader to walk or run in a variety of directions. On a signal by the leader, the person at the end of each line (file) sprints to the front of the line and becomes the new leader. Continue until everyone have had at least one turn as the leader

 It's a stretch…strong and flexible muscles will perform better

Cooling Down

Once completing your family walk or run together, finish with a few cool-down stretches similar to the ones during warm-ups. Remember that while walking or running continuously is natural for most active children, they can always benefit from their mom's and dad's genuine guidance and care. Keep it fun, keep it simple, bring a water bottle along and enjoy your time together for a lifetime.

Kids' Marathon—One Kilometre at a Time

THE STRATEGY IS SIMPLE AND FUN.

WHAT?

Walk or run 41.2 K prior to a marathon event. Finish the final kilometre on the day of the actual marathon event day. You can do this in your neighbourhood or at the kids/family fun run event usually held at most marathon festivals.

This strategy can be completed as a family together, as individual family members or by your children. Can be encouraged for many event distances as well, e.g., 5, 10, 21.1 kilometre or ultra events. The strategy promotes consistent daily or three times per week walk/run playout sessions.

GOAL?

Walk/run 41.2 K plus one kilometre on event day = 42.2 K (marathon distance).

HOW?

Choose a calendar to record the actual marathon event day/date that Mom and or Dad are preparing for. Assist your children to decide how often they are going to run their one kilometre prior to your event day, e.g., can decide to run every day for 42 days prior to the event day or one kilometer three times per week or whatever makes sense for your children and you. Every day that they get out for a one kilometre walk or run log the date and the distance on a calendar, including Mom's and or Dad's training distances as well. Try to walk or run with your children as they do their one kilometre walk or run. You'll be okay as you prepare and build on your distances.

TRAINING TIPS?

- **complete the program gradually— you are encouraging consistent walk or run outings**

- **start with shorter distances as necessary and building to the one kilometre distance**

- **walk or run with a parent, a friend, a neighbour, extended family member**

- **distance—one kilometre is about 10 city blocks**

- **take your time, find your "talking" pace, have many fun one kilometre walk or runs**

CELEBRATION?

Support and cheer and encourage everyone along during their training period. Event Day—be at the finish line for each other—children at Mom and Dad marathon finish line; Mom and Dad at their children's final one kilometre finish line. Pictures together, loud cheers and high-fives all around!

Sounds like a great strategy for a lifetime of marathons—one kilometre at a time.

Chapter 4
Running Tips

Stretching Tips

1. Calf

- Stand about a metre from a wall, rail or tree.
- Place your feet flat on the ground, toes slightly turned inward.
- Bend your forward leg.
- Keep your opposite leg back and straight and feel the tension in the calf.
- Bend the straight leg at the knee to work the Achilles tendon.

2. Quadriceps

- Place one arm on a wall or rail to help balance yourself (if needed).
- Use the other hand to pull the foot back.
- The bent knee should touch the other knee.
- To protect the back, pull your abdominal muscles in with a pelvic tilt.
- Watch your alignment, heel back toward your buttocks, knees together.
- Stretch, breathe and relax.
- Repeat with your other leg.

3. Iliotibial Band Stretch

- **Stand parallel to a wall, an arm's length away.**
- **With feet together, extend your arm sideways, wrist bent, with your palm against the wall.**
- **Lean toward the wall with your opposite hand on the outside of your hip.**
- **Breathe in and out with your legs straight.**
- **Tighten your buttocks and push your hips toward the wall.**
- **Push, feeling the stretch on the outside of the leg nearest the wall.**
- **Hold the stretch—breathe and relax.**
- **Repeat on the other leg.**

4. Groin

- **Sit upright with your back straight.**
- **Sit with knees up, and then let them drop open to the sides with the soles of your shoes facing each other.**
- **With your hands on your ankles, pull your feet toward your buttocks.**
- **Rest your arms on the insides of your legs.**
- **Gently push your knees toward the ground.**
- **Feel the stretch in your groin area, breathe and relax.**

5. Hamstring

- Lie flat on your back.
- Raise one leg on the doorway, corner or tree.
- Your other leg should be flat on the ground.
- With breathing relaxed and both legs straight, do not bend your knee.
- You can increase the stretch by moving your butt closer to the doorway or tree.
- Hold the stretch and relax.
- Repeat with your other leg.

6. Lower Back

- Lie flat on your back with your legs straight out.
- Bring your bent knees up to your chest.
- Grasp your legs behind the knees.
- Keep your knees together.
- Gently pull your knees to your chest.
- Keep your back flat on the ground.
- Breathe, hold the stretch and relax.

7. Hip Flexor

- Kneel on one knee and place the other forward at a 90-degree stance.
- Keep your back straight and maintain a pelvic tilt.
- The rear knee is planted to stretch the hip in front.
- Keep your knee on the ground and shift your hips forward.
- You should feel the stretch in the hip of the rear leg.
- Switch legs and repeat.

8. Buttock Stretch

- Sit up straight with one leg straight out and the knee of the other leg bent.
- Put the foot of the bent leg on the outside of the straightened leg.
- Slowly bend the leg toward the opposing shoulder.
- Feel the stretch high in the hip and buttock area of the bent leg.
- Hold the stretch, breathe and relax.

Breathing

Breathing, the simple act of inhaling and exhaling, can be complicated. Much like running, the act of putting one foot in front of the other is a lot more complicated than one would expect. Watch the super-talented singer who has mastered breathing. This mastery allows him or her to hit and hold the long high notes. Better yet, look at swimmers who have mastered breathing, if for no other reason than they do not want to get a mouthful of water. As runners we occasionally get caught up in our sport and forget some basics like breathing. We start our runs in a race or group environment and the excitement causes us to breath high in our chest, rather than "belly" breathing. The short, high breathing can cause us to hyperventilate or get the dreaded "runner's stitch." Here are some tips that will make your stitch go away and get you more relaxed in your breathing, thereby allowing you to run faster.

Stand up tall, shoulders back and put one hand on your belly. Purse your lips and fully exhale. When we fully exhale we do not need to think about breathing in, as nature does this as part of our survival technique. We breathe in relaxed and "belly breathe" when we fully exhale. This deep breathing is both more relaxed and more efficient in the use of oxygen. Keep your breathing relaxed, deep, rhythmic and in time with your running stride by concentrating on fully exhaling. Inhale in a relaxed, full, deep breath. So now as you run, concentrate on the upper body being relaxed and rhythmic with the power of your running focused on your hip down. The initial power is coming from the push off of the ankle and the glide and relaxed lift of the knee coming from the hip flexors. Save the huffing and puffing for the big bad wolf stories. Now you know why one of the most common things a coach gets athletes to concentrate on is to relax. The more relaxed you are the higher the level of performance.

Form

1. STAY UPRIGHT

Good running posture is simply good body posture. When the head, shoulders and hips are all lined up over the feet, you can move forward as a unit with a minimum amount of effort.

2. CHEST FORWARD

Many runners let their chest sag into a slouch. In such a position, the lungs won't maximize their efficiency. Before starting your run, relax and take a deep breath, which moves the lungs into an efficient position. After you exhale, maintain the chest in this beneficial alignment. The most efficient way to run is to have your head, neck and shoulders erect. When you run leaning forward, you're always fighting gravity.

3. HIPS FORWARD

One of the most common errors of form is letting the hips shift back and the butt stick out behind you. Taking a deep breath often pulls the hips forward into an alignment that allows easier running.

4. THE FOOT PLANT

There is a difference between what should happen and what you may be able to control. First, let your shoe professional fit you with a couple of pairs of shoes that are right for you. Then, just start running! Your personal stride is the result of your shape, your physique, and the strength and balance of your muscles, at least all the way up to your waist! Please don't try to change your foot plant as you train: you will not be running naturally, and you are very likely to cause more problems than you solve. Changes to your gait only happen as a result of long-term changes elsewhere. As you gain fitness and strength, you may notice that many irregularities resolve themselves. Modern training shoes are designed to accommodate biomechanically different feet. Maybe the problem you thought you had will turn out to be not so much of a problem after all. But if you really do have a problem that continues to affect your activity, you may have to seek the advice of a therapist or coach to assess and deal with your particular situation.

5. ARMS

The starting position for arms in all running is to have them hanging vertically and loosely from the shoulders. From this starting position, arm carriage varies depending on what form of running you're doing. But your shoulders should always be low and relaxed. In active walking and in "long arm" power walking, the full length of the arm will swing. The swing will be gentle in active walking, and more dynamic and march-like in power walking. In "short arm" power walking and race walking, the arms are bent at the elbow. Usually, the arms are at a 90-degree angle in the starting position. If you are power walking, you can keep the angle at 90 degrees throughout. If you do, you will notice that your hand tends to go upwards when the arm is behind you. That's a strong, dynamic action that will work on your upper body as well. In race walking, we need our upper body to be a little "quieter" and to work "forward and back" rather than "up and down."

6. STRIDE RATE, NOT STRIDE LENGTH

Studies have shown that when runners get faster, the stride length actually decreases, but the stride rate ("turnover" in athletes' jargon) increases. Too long a stride results in three problems. First, the big secret of an athletically efficient gait is that the foot is already moving backwards when it hits the ground. When your foot is stuck out in front of you, that's not happening. Second, with too long a stride, we land at a point coaches call "ahead of the body's centre of mass." It's like putting on a brake; we have to wait until our foot is directly under the body before we start pushing forward again. Shorten the stride and we land more or less under the body already. Third, extra time in the air is largely wasted: when our feet aren't on the ground, they're not driving us forward.

Unless you are naturally endowed with a long stride that is already efficient, improvements in your own personal efficiency are likely to come first from shortening your stride. Lengthening your stride naturally is a long-term process of increased fitness and muscle strengthening. The results of all this biomechanics is that when you "overstride" the muscles work harder than they need to. They will tighten up and tire before your run is done. The fatigue will make you soon revert to your natural stride length anyway.

7. HEAD AND NECK

Your torso will normally do what your head is doing. So if you are dropping your head right down, your torso will probably follow and lean too far forward. Keep the neck and shoulders relaxed. Try not to hunch your shoulders. This position will cause undue fatigue to that area. Your eyes should be looking somewhere about 20 to 30 metres ahead of you.

8. PRACTICE TWICE A WEEK

Once or twice a week, a little technique work is really helpful. After your warm-up, run some accelerations of 50 to 150 metres. Pick one of the elements of good form and feel yourself executing it well during the acceleration. Rehearse each element at least four times, and keep to one or two elements at most in each session. A change in technique may feel a little awkward at first, but you'll know when you've got it right—it feels so good! In technique work, the short periods are the key. When you're moving your body in a new way, your brain literally gets tired, and quite quickly too! You'll feel when it happens; there will be a noticeable loss in your "coordination." It's temporary; the short break between accelerations will give you the recovery you need. If you take up race walking, there will be a little more emphasis on technique. Efficient technique gains precious speed and resists the effects of fatigue.

Chapter 5

Active and Healthy All Year Long

How Active and Healthy Is Your Family?

Take a few minutes to go through this questionnaire (adapted from www.dailythingscount.ca) as a family or individually. It is a quick reminder of the healthy habits you can feel pretty good about. Just answer "yes" or "no" out loud or to yourself.

ACTIVE HABITS
As a family, together or individually

○ we get 60 to 90 minutes of physical activity each day

○ we play outside every day (both children and adults)

○ we try a variety of different activities and sports

○ we have fun while we are active

○ we control our daily screen time

○ we are active together most days of the week

NUTRITION HABITS
As a family, together or individually

○ we eat breakfast to start each day

○ we include foods from all four food groups from *Canada's Food Guide*

○ we eat at least four servings of vegetables and fruits each day

○ we eat the right *Canada's Food Guide* serving sizes most of the time

○ we eat together at least three times a week

○ we eat homemade lunches

○ we eat at home most days

OTHER HEALTHY HABITS
As a family, together or individually

○ the parents are excellent role models for making healthy and active choices their only choices every day

○ we get the right amount of sleep each night (8 hours or more)

○ we support each other's healthy eating and physical activity habits

○ we give each other a shoulder to lean on in times of mental stress and need

○ we share our healthy habits and with our extended family: relatives, friends, colleagues, neighbours

---

Post this questionnaire on your refrigerator door or another high-traffic area in your home. It can be a reminder and motivator for everyone. Can you think of a few more healthy habits to add?

Wherever an individual or the family answered "no," decide how everyone can come together to make a few small changes to eventually get to a "yes" answer. Set a goal to support each other to make the change happen.

Healthy Choices

OVERWEIGHT FAMILY MEMBERS

Be supportive, provide encouragement and ensure acceptance. Help each other learn new strategies to maintain a healthy weight. Focus on good health and not just weight. This attitude is not an issue of how one might look but and issue of good health. Being overweight affects health and may lead to chronic disease in the future. Family should be the focus—everyone models the healthy behaviour, not just the individual experiencing the challenge. Make gradual changes to the family's physical activity and eating habits.

EAT HEALTHIER AT HOME

Start your day with a healthy family breakfast. Plan for snacks of vegetables and fruit rather than pop and chips. How about trading in and using a salad plate rather than a dinner plate to encourage smaller portions. Start with lighter salads and vegetables, which have lower calories, before continuing to the correct portion for meats. Try preparing foods in a variety of ways—baking, roasting and broiling—using a variety of healthy oils.

RANDOM ACTS OF EXERCISE

Do you feel like you don't always have time to be active? Try some random acts of exercise. Any time is a good time, especially if you've been sitting at school, work or home for a while. Instead of hiding your home exercise equipment, bring it into a room you are in most of the time. Read while you walk or run on a treadmill; ride a stationary bike and watch your favourite movie or bike workout. Think of TV as an exercise box. Exercise during commercials or between programs. Keep an exercise log handy. Count every step you take with a pedometer on those walks and runs all the way to 10,000 steps. Walk to the corner store, library or friend's home.

NEIGHBOURHOOD PHYSICAL ACTIVITY

If parents think their neighbourhood is safe, clean and walkable and has public parks and other green spaces for all to play in, then their children are more likely to be playing outside throughout the year. Involve a variety of adult neighbours in taking turns to supervise and of course participate with active children outside in their neighbourhoods.

Winter Active

Don't let shorter days, colder temperatures and challenging winter conditions stop you from burning calories, increasing your cardiovascular fitness and strengthening your muscles by continuing to be active outside. Outdoor activity during the winter months is also wonderful for your mental health by helping beat those winter blues. The perfect combination of outdoor activity in the sunshine will assist to elevate our mood and attitude.

Families that spend more time outside at any time of the year tend to be more active in general. We are fortunate in our Canadian winter climate to experience the wonders of a beautiful winter walk after or during a fresh snowfall, making the first footprints, building a snowman, skating on an outdoor rink, tobogganing or shovelling our walkways to create a huge mound of snow for creative minds to mend and manipulate into something to play on or in. Just think, many children and families around the world don't experience this opportunity to be active in the snow and cold during the winter months. Let's be thankful and embrace these snowy months outside as much as we actively can. You know it's not as bad when you get outside as it looked when you and your family were inside.

Try a few new activities. If you enjoy walking and running, try snowshoeing and cross-country skiing on snowy tails or open fields. How about downhill skiing and snowboarding? One of the benefits of advances in technology is that all of the new equipment is lighter in weight, shorter in length and therefore easier to play with. Rentals, lessons and assistance plans for participation are available in most communities. Ice skates are lighter, more comfortable and available in many colours. Get outside for a skate in the fresh cool air rather than an indoor rink. Don't forget to play safely, take lessons, wear a helmet for skating and skiing and dress in layers to protect yourself from frostbite or hypothermia.

Dress in layers with all parts of the body covered to enhance everyone's safe exposure and enjoyment during colder weather patterns. A temperature check might be minus 20 to minus 23 degrees Celsius, with no significant wind, as safe outdoor play temperatures for everyone. Include a buddy system to check each other for frostbite on exposed skin areas. Play close to home or in parks and other locations that have access to indoor shelters or buildings.

Have everyone brainstorm the outdoor winter activities that can reasonably be provided by your family. Post the list on your activity board and see how often you can get out over the winter months to try as many of the activities as possible.

Here are a few ideas adapted and modified from Active Healthy Kids Canada (**www.activehealthykids.ca**).

COOL AND FROSTY WALKS

Capture a breath of fresh air by taking a walk around your neighbourhood. Enjoy the festive decorations and lights that are common during the holiday season. To add some fun, have every family member estimate the time it will take to reach a particular destination and then compare their estimates to the actual time you are out.

WINTER LOOKOUT

Take a pencil and small writing pad on your walks to remember or record the variety of winter features that we only usually see at this time of the year: chimney exhaust, snow, ice, winter birds, animal tracks (including pets and human), which trees are still green and which are not. Can you see anything else that is unique to this time of the year?

FAMILY SNOW PILE

This activity can be done as one group or in teams of whatever number makes sense for the size of your family. Invite friends along, too. Go to a large, snow-filled open space, schoolyard or park. Each family team has five minutes to build the highest snow pile. They can only use their hands and legs. A variation of this game is to build a snowman or other creative snow sculpture.

SNOW SHOVEL–SNOWBALL RELAYS

Break up into teams, each with a snow shovel and a snowball. Line up team members one behind the other. The first person from each team starts carrying the snowball with the shovel. They walk, run, ski or skate around a marker placed a few metres away and back to the start. The next team member takes the snow shovel and snowball and completes the same course. If the snowball falls it must be picked up with the snow shovel only—no hands. You can vary the course with obstacles, different styles of movement—walk, run, skip, hop or gallop—or you can flip and catch the snowball as you are moving. If the snowball is solid enough, use your feet to move it along. Repeat as many times as possible.

SLED RACES

"Mushers" take turns being pulled on a sled or toboggan by their family team of "dogs" around a marked course. Schoolyards, parks or any other open, snowy field is perfect for mushing.

More Active Winter Ideas

- Build a snow fort.
- Bundle up and make snow angels or other creative designs.
- Go ice fishing.
- Explore different off-leash parks with a dog and observe its snow tracks.
- Go for a walk and count how many birds and other animals are active.
- Too cold outside? Go for a walk in a mall or indoor playground.
- Organize a winter walking school bus in your neighbourhood.

- Build snow stairs into the side of a hill. Walk up and slide down.
- Play snow soccer, football or baseball.
- Create an outdoor snowy obstacle course at a school playground.
- Get shovels for the whole family to help shovel the sidewalks and steps in your neighbourhood.
- Play a family or neighbourhood street hockey game before watching a game on TV.
- Create a family winter triathlon using any three outdoor activities (e.g., snowshoe, skate, walk, run, ski).

Family Winter Olympics

During a Winter Olympic and Paralympic year, consider learning more about and trying as many of the games' winter sports. Use websites or your local library to find illustrations and descriptions of the various of sports. Some are familiar, like hockey, skiing, figure skating and curling, but other may not be. How about luge, skeleton, speed skating, half pipe snowboarding, free style skiing or sledge hockey? How do wheelchair athletes compete in curling?

Many of the sports will have local clubs or provincial contacts. Take your family to a local curling rink, receive a few tips and lessons and then enjoy a few ends of this great game. Start your own neighbourhood brier. Learn to speed skate, cross-country ski, downhill ski or snowboard at local facilities. Most have reasonably priced learning programs to provide new exposure to their activities.

If you search around your community you will be pleasantly surprised at what you might find to liven up your Olympic/Paralympic spirit. It's time to organize an Olympic day or week of new activities and sports for your family and friends.

Creating and participating in your own Winter Olympic circuit will surely invigorate our wellness during these winter months. Choose a series of outdoor activities to be done one after the other. Try some of the one described here or have everyone brainstorm their own ideas. Invite another family or friends along. Remember, hot chocolate is mandatory.

OLYMPIC TORCH RUN

You have to start each family outing with a family torch run with flashlights during the early evening to get the full effect. Everyone walks, runs or wheels together in a straight line or takes turns walking a pre-planned route. Invite neighbours or friends—you could always have active spectators cheering along the way before they take their turn at the torch run.

Pull a torch carrier in a toboggan or put on snowshoes or cross-country skis for an extra challenge. Go down to the local outdoor community rink and skate the torch around the rink a few times, followed by many skate type challenges that everyone can participate in.

ALPINE SKIING OVER LINES

What would it be like to be a downhill skier? To find out, just make a straight line in the snow by walking heel to toe for a few meters. Have family members jump with two feet from side to side, back and forth over the line. Set your ski course up at a local park or schoolyard that has a rolling hill(s). Include a slalom course by jumping and travelling forward in a zigzag pattern along the line or just anywhere in the play area. Remember, try to move like a downhill skier, nice and low, turning and jumping with your feet together. Use ski poles if you have them.

SKI JUMPING

Imagine you're a ski jumper soaring through the cool, wintry air. Start at the top of a small rise. Crouch low, with both boots together and your gloves touching the snow. On the count of three, jump as high as you can and comfortably land on both feet about shoulder width apart. Hold that position for a few more seconds before you imagine coming to a complete stop at the bottom of the hill. Try three or four more ski jumps. Try to land a little further down the hill each time. After a few stationary jumps, try running and jumping for height and landing comfortably on both feet.

PAIRS FIGURE SKATING

What would it feel like to be a figure skater? Jumping and turning and stopping and starting and balancing and doing cross over steps on my skates. Play with a family member or friend by taking turns mirroring each others' movements through the snow. Move through the play area by taking long smooth walking or running strides. Put on music and create your own pairs routines. Take turns being the mirror.

CROSS-COUNTRY SKIING

What do the traditional Nordic skiing or skate skiing events look like? I'm sure it won't be hard to find a slippery section on your sidewalk. Try sliding your boots from side to side for skate skiing or front to back for Nordic skiing. Swing your arms using imaginary poles. How do the pole plants differ for your arm actions? There are speed events and endurance events, so get your feet moving very quickly for one minute and then in long, slow, controlled slides for a few minutes to get that distance in for your endurance.

IT'S BRIER TIME

Now it's your turn to be an Olympic curler coming out of the hack. Choose an object to throw underhand along the snow (e.g., a rubber chicken, softball or snowball). Try performing a series of long, slow forward lunges while moving forward. Hold your balance for a few seconds between each lunge. Other family members can clear the way by sweeping—with a household broom—a space for your object to travel. Try three or four lunges and throws one after the other; then switch and sweep for a while.

TOBOGGANING FOR GOLD

Luge, skeleton and bobsled are some of the most exciting events at the Olympics. Pick up your family toboggan or slider and head for a local hill or rise in a schoolyard or park—somewhere safe in terms of height and steepness. Helmets and goggles might be a good idea, and keep the sliding area separate from where you walk up the hill. Make sure everyone is at the bottom before making your way back up.

Luge is performed by sitting feet first on your toboggan. Give yourself a few good pushes and pulls with your hands and arms. When you are underway, lay down on the toboggan with your head slightly up to enjoy the ride down. Try shifting your weight back and forth to create long slow turns. It will feel exhilarating.

For the **skeleton** event you lie down on your front, headfirst. For a running start, place both hands on either side of the toboggan or slider, take a few running steps then lower yourself onto the toboggan with your arms at your sides. Keep your eyes open and let out a loud "Yahoo" as you skeleton down the hill. Shift your weight back and forth to make a few turns. Now you know why you need a helmet and goggles.

Are you ready for the **bobsled**? It's a fun ride with all family members on the toboggan. In teams of two or four you run and jump together onto the toboggan. One person will be the driver at the front and one the brake person at the back. Try swaying slowly together from side to side, working as one unit to feel the turns of the run. Now this is a family team ride!

FUN WITH BIATHLON

Biathlon involves cross-country skiing and shooting at targets along the course. You can mimic this sport on your winter walks, runs or skis. Schoolyards or parks are great locations to set a course through the snow. Stop every so often and choose an appropriate target—fence, tree, backstop or anything else that won't be damaged or considered vandalism. Make a few snowballs or take a few balls from home and try to hit the target from a few meters away. Try throwing from a standing position for some of the targets, from kneeling or from lying down on your front.

Create a biathlon course with five or more suitable targets. See how quickly everyone can walk, run or ski through the course and how accurately you can hit the targets with your snowballs. Give everyone five throws at each target. How many times did you hit the target? Keep a family total.

OLYMPIC HOCKEY

Clear a ball hockey area on your street (closed to traffic), go down to the local outdoor community rink or find a safe pond or frozen lake for a rousing game of hockey. It won't take much imagination to get going for gold with this event. Get the neighbourhood out to create a few country teams to play each other. How many total goals can each team score through all of their games?

WHERE IS THAT HOT CHOCOLATE?

Family winter outdoor play is priceless. Enjoy the winter months together watching, supporting and playing your way through the next Winter Olympic or Paralympic Games.

Family Vacation

The next time you are fortunate to plan a winter getaway with your family, consider including and planning for extra physical activity opportunities. Everyone will feel better when they return home if you maintained your usual routines of daily physical activity and healthy eating as much as possible.

If you can, stay in accommodations that offer various types of activity lessons—tennis, golf, cycling, scuba, snorkelling, skiing and many others. Large cities might offer walking tours, visits to the zoo, museums, parks and cycling tours that all rely on your own active transport. Don't forget about the fitness centre and everything it has to offer, including that steam, sauna or hot tub to end your active day.

Vacation packages for families on cruise ships will cater to children of all ages. From wall climbing to pools to walks around the variety of ship decks there are many opportunities to stay active. Ever wonder what its like to run on a moving ship? Try it.

One of the challenges on cruises is the non-stop access to food. Try not to break the pattern of healthy nutritious eating that everyone has worked on. Consider six smaller meals through the day rather than three larger meals. You only require small amounts of each of the four food groups to keep you going. One of the positives is that on vacations we usually sit together for family meals.

Summer Active

Encouraging children to be active during the summer months can be challenging for many families. Your goal of creating or continuing a healthy and active environment in our homes and neighbourhoods needs to continue after school gets out. Parents can come together in the neighbourhood to develop daily active and nutritious plans for their children. Resources can be found at schools, local libraries, health units and family leisure centres. Online resources provided by Health Canada are excellent and provide many useful links to other reputable agencies for both daily physical activity and healthy eating ideas and strategies.

Here are a few suggestions for your daily active and nutritious plans:

- Set regular times during the week for family play.
- Enjoy a family walk after dinner.
- Walk to the library and other daily routines.
- Enter a community fun walk or run.
- Go for a hike on a trail in a park, up and down rolling hills.
- Enter a community triathlon: swim, cycle, walk/run.
- Start a walking or running club in your community.
- Wake up and play with yoga.
- Create a fun obstacle course through a neighbourhood playground.
- Encourage unstructured or free play: street hockey, baseball, tennis, tag games, rope skipping, climbing, and throwing, catching and kicking.
- Walk or run a marathon, one kilometre at a time for 42 consecutive days.

- Walk or run a neighbourhood treasure hunt.
- Walk your dog or a friend's or neighbour's at least twice a day.
- Include physical activities in birthdays, family gatherings or when friends come over to visit.
- Search out the local orienteering association for weekly family events. Bring another family with yours.
- Try a new activity like wall or rock climbing, snorkelling, scuba diving, yoga or a variety of dance type classes.

Individually or as a family, keep a diary of what you did every day to have an active summer. Parents can use these diaries to help decide what works and what doesn't to get their family more healthy and active. And at the end of the summer you can read your diaries together to help remember the great summer moments you had as an active family.

Family Summer Olympics

The Olympic motto is made up of three Latin words: citius, altius, fortius (faster, higher, stronger). These words are meant to inspire athletes to give their best performances during competition. Your family can use this motto through the summer months as everyone strives on a daily basis to make only healthy and active lifestyle choices. You should value and recognize a variety of levels of excellence by encouraging family members to try as best as they can during play or in their daily routines. As each Olympic summer approaches, let's use the Olympics as our "flame" to continue improving and motivating ourselves toward our own ideal family moments.

Involve all family members in the decision-making about the types of activities and nutritional choices that they want to try and be involved in. Solve problems and set goals together. Give your children opportunities to demonstrate their proficiency in the activities of their choice or the healthy snacks and meals they prepare during any given day.

Here are some suggestions that can make your Olympic moments shine:

- Contact a local or provincial Olympic or Paralympic association to ask about sport demonstrations or active tryout sessions. There are dozens of Olympic and Paralympic sports, so get out and try a few as family outings.

- Adopt an Olympic athlete or team from your community, province or country. Try to make contact with that athlete or team through a provincial or national sports association. Try their sport, if you haven't already. Rally your neighbours, school or community at large. Maybe you can get your Olympic athlete or team to visit before or after their Summer Olympics or Paralympics.

- Walk or run an Olympic marathon at one kilometer a day for 42 consecutive days. Conclude with a special event (e.g., local race event). How long would it take for your family to walk or run to the next Summer Olympics location?

- Create an active family movie. Have a family member produce a video of parents, siblings, pets, friends, neighbours and themselves being active together or individually. Add the Olympic music or your own as a soundtrack.

- Plan to have at least one day a week as a non-electronics day. Go for a day without using computers, TV, radio, smart phones, tablets or the family vehicle. How are you going to prepare your healthy family snacks and meals with no electricity?

- Organize a community league health fair. Let all children help choose the sessions that make up the fair. Many community-based support services would be willing to come out for free to provide sessions, set up displays or provide demonstrations. Sessions could include local Olympic sport displays and active sessions, community nurses, dieticians, healthy snacks for Olympic athletes, dance sessions, yoga, Pilates, safe communities and first aid. It's a great way to bring your community together.

- Create an active mentor program in your community. Match older, responsible youth with younger children. Mentors can role model healthy lifestyles for younger children and organize community activities. They can help divide all of the children into balanced teams, have each team adopt a country and choose a variety of Olympic sports for few friendly games. Try to change the Olympic sports each week. Parents or other adults can be included on teams. A children versus adults game could be highlighted at the end of each summer week.

- Try a few Olympic racquet sports, such as tennis, badminton or table tennis. Singles or doubles can be played. It's a great way to make use of those outdoor courts or school and community gymnasiums over the summer. Each individual or team can adopt to represent an Olympic country. Get an old T-shirt and colour and print the country's flag on the front with your family member's name on the back.

- Don't forget, Olympic athletes need to prepare nutritious snacks and meals for energy. Organize healthy cooking sessions at your community league facility. Invite children and parents to share their own recipes from their Olympic country.

- Challenge another nearby community or family to a friendly activity competition. Each family team can set fitness and nutrition goals and then attempt to meet or beat their goals. If one family team does not meet their goals, then that community league president or family member must wear the Olympic T-shirt of the other community family group.

- Do a little research together as a family to see what kinds of footwear the Olympic athletes wear for their sport. We know what soccer and basketball players wear, but what about a shot putter, equestrian athlete, rower, sprinter, lawn bowler, javelin thrower, field hockey goalie or mountain biker? Each family member chooses a unique type of footwear and draws it on a large sheet of paper. Then they cut it out and post it on a wall. Every time they are active they record the activity and duration on their Olympic shoe. You could also colour in a portion of the shoe after each activity. When it's all coloured in, join in for a family cheer or help another family member to fill up their shoe with activity, too.

- Organize a community Summer Olympics or Paralympics of your own. Divide all participants into teams according to countries. They are responsible for creating their own flag and uniform as well as choosing a team anthem from their adopted country or a favourite pop song. Hold an opening ceremony during the evening with a flashlight torch walk to introduce the teams, the competition structure and the rules of the sporting events. Try to choose sports that are not usually played in the community. Contact local Olympic associations for assistance. Give out awards for sportsmanship, fair play and team spirit. At the closing ceremonies, present the awards and play the team anthems. Finish the day with a healthy community potluck of Olympic portions.

Active Summer Camp

If summer camp options are a must for your family, look for opportunities at your local community centres or nearby colleges or universities. Many community agencies provide monetary assistance for families. Outreach programs are provided to many rural settings. Contact your local or provincial sport organization for more information.

One of the recent new features of summer camps is to include not only sport-specific camps, such as soccer, basketball, baseball or hockey, but also all-inclusive camps that introduce children to a variety of activities throughout the day or duration of the camp. For instance, camps may include ultimate Frisbee, wall climbing, water activities, hip-hop dance, orienteering or racquet activities, to name only a few. What a great way to spend a day or week, engaged in physical activity that may be new to your active children.

Some camp organizers feed their participants a healthy lunch and snacks, as well. Sounds like a wonderful active daycare to me!

Chapter 6
Active Family Fun

Active Adventures

Active family fun is valuable time together that should be treasured. Plan a few family adventures by visiting—on foot and public transportation—the sights of your community in your immediate neighbourhood and across town. Try hiking, fishing, canoeing or going to a self pick berry or veggie farm. Discover public parks, visit the zoo or explore other outdoor attractions. Be a tourist in your own community for a day and visit places you haven't yet been to or go to infrequently.

Plan an active get away. Swim at a supervised beach or outdoor community pool or bike on a scenic trail. Hike or camp in a provincial, state or national park. Raft down a river or take a walking tour of a city you are visiting.

Volunteer as a family to help others while benefitting yourselves. Help your neighbours in their yards, do litter patrol in your community, clean up a favourite park or schoolyard or enter a walk or run charity event as a family.

Every Minute Counts

Families trying to provide a comfortable standard of living are constantly squeezed for time, money and the cost of services. But everything you can do to keep a healthy active lifestyle belongs at the top of your individual and family "to do" lists. Now, more than ever, daily physical activity and healthy eating are key ingredients that will help all family members with their mental fitness and with handling the stress of work, school and extra-curricular schedules.

From daycare to high school, the boardroom to various workplaces, it's all of those little things—both movement and nutritional—that will continue to make a difference for family health and well being. Active transport—travelling under your own steam—to and from work or school, the park, the corner store or a friend's place are little things that will enhance everyone's steps per day. Active transport plus public transport equals healthy transport.

Including one more servings of colourful fruits and vegetables each day is another little thing that can be economically managed. Daily healthy eating plus daily physical activity equals healthy booster shots for parents at work or home and for children at school.

Shorter day light hours should not translate into less time for all the things you do as a family. The perfect "gym" for your family is the one you can provide at your own indoor and outdoor spaces, it's economical too—no gym fees. Children and adults play in the form of walking, running, wheeling of cycling.

Daily family physical activity plus daily personal physical activity should equal a minimum of 30 minutes. This activity can be done all at once or by repeating active minutes throughout the day. It should be enjoyable time and not added stressful time.

Turn on the music and consider adding healthy active minute enhancers at school, work, home or outdoors.

ONE MINUTE
Do a few simple head-to-toe stretches and movements while sitting or standing. Enjoy a glass of water after each series of these minutes.

THREE MINUTES
Walk, run, skip, hop, dance or perform other aerobic activities on the spot or as space allows for one minute. Do simple head to toe stretches or movements for one minute. Now, do a new aerobic activity for one minute. Enjoy a glass of water after each.

FIVE MINUTES
Do any aerobic activity on the spot or around the space for two minutes. Do simple head to toe stretches or movements for one minute. Do your own body weight strength activities—push-ups, curl-ups, body planks, jumping jacks, double leg squats—for one minute. Follow it up with any aerobic activity for one minute. Enjoy a glass of water.

TEN MINUTES
Do at least two or more aerobic activities for three minutes, followed by simple head to toe stretches or movements for two minutes. Perform your own body strength activities for two minutes. Finish with two or more aerobic activities for three minutes. Enjoy one very large glass of water or more.

Tag Games

Tag is an excellent activity to use as a warm-up because tag games are active, usually have few rules, are very inclusive, practice many physical literacy basic skills for a variety of movements, including walking, running, skipping, galloping, changing directions, balance, stopping and starting, increasing heart rate and breathing and typically do not take a long time to set up and get playing.

Change tag games frequently to ensure interest remains high and that everyone has a chance to be tagged or a tagger. Many of the tag games included do not have specific names, so let everyone take turns naming a few and making up a few new family-owned tag games.

You don't need a new game every day, but a variety of games keeps interest high without too much repetition. Come back to a game in a few months or reserve a few games for various seasons of the year. When a number of families are together, play the games that are fun with larger numbers. Play the smaller, shorter games when just your own family gets to play. are together, play the games that are fun with larger numbers. Play the smaller, shorter games when just your own family gets to play.

ⓘ There are many online and hardcopy resources to choose from. Many of these suggestions are adapted from *Everybody Play,* by Arndt and Loscher (1990) and *Fundamental Motor Skills*, by the Victoria Department of Education in Australia (1998).

PAIRS TAG

Participants: Eight or more.

PLAY AREA: Players decide size and irregular shape.
RULES: If someone in the chasing group releases their hands, they cannot catch or tag the others.
DESCRIPTION: Start with one family pair of players with joined hands trying to catch or tag other individual players. When they tag a player, that player now joins hands to increase the size of the chasing group. The game ends when all individual players have been caught or tagged and everyone makes one large family group.

ROCKET/RACE CAR BLAST OFF

Participants: One or more.

PLAY AREA: Large, open green space.
EQUIPMENT: Objects to indicate start and finish lines.
DESCRIPTION: Talk each other through a variety of creative "blast off" actions. Take turns after each blast off.
"Engine Starting": running on the spot slowly.
"Engine is Warming": running on the spot quicker.
"Engine is Revving Louder": running on the spot with high knees.
"5,4,3,2,1 Blast Off": running on the spot with high knees and then sprinting to the finish line.

SHADOW TAG

Participants: Four or more.

PLAY AREA: Players decide size and boundary.
RULES: A player is safe in the shade.
DESCRIPTION: Have a player volunteer to be It. It chases a player and tries to tag them by stepping on their shadow. When tagged, they exchange roles. This game is suitable for ages four and up. Of course, a bright sunny day is required for this game.

ONE PERSON CATCHES THE OTHER

Participants: Two or more.

PLAY AREA: Green space marked with natural or player made boundaries. Vary size of play area according to numbers of and age of participants. Try to vary the boundaries from straight sides to uneven sides and shapes.
RULES: Players are in family groups of two or three and all stay in the same playing area.
DESCRIPTION: The players take turns trying to catch each other. After a player is caught, the new catcher lets the player run away. Players can walk, run or use other types of movement (e.g., skip, gallop).

VARIATION: The catcher holds a ball, pool noodle or other soft object with both hands and has to friendly-touch the other player with it. Or, in a narrow play area, each player hops on one leg or both legs or runs on both hands and feet.

POISON TAG

Participants: Four or more.

PLAY AREA: Players decide size and boundary.
DESCRIPTION: Have a player volunteer to be It. When players are tagged by It, they must place their hand over the body part that was tagged and continue to run away. The strategy is for It to tag players as low on their body as possible (e.g., ankle or foot) to make it difficult for them to run. The round ends when one player is immobilized. That player becomes It for the next round.

FOUR CORNERS

Participants: Four or more.

PLAY AREA: Open grassy area with irregular boundaries.

EQUIPMENT: Bean bags, pieces of cloth, scarves, gloves, anything else to pick up.

DESCRIPTION: Place objects in four corners of the play area. Individuals or family teams of equal numbers start in their designated corners. On a signal "Go," players from each family team run out of their own corner to the other corners and pick up an object to bring back to their own corner. They can only collect one object at a time and cannot protect their own objects from being taken from their own corner. Play for a short period of time, then stop and have each team count the number of objects they have collected in their corner.

VARIATIONS: Dribble the objects (a variety of ball sizes) with your feet under control back to corner; use a hockey stick to move the objects; have family teams change corners after each stoppage in play.

RUN/WALK AWAY

Participants: Two or more.

PLAY AREA: Open green space.

DESCRIPTION: One player is the caller. Players stand very close to the caller (e.g., arm's-length away). On the signal "Go," players walk or run as quickly as possible away from the caller until the caller says, "Stop." The players then walk back to the caller. On "Go," the players try to get as far away as they can from the caller. The caller varies the time in which they say, "Stop."

VARIATION: Switch callers and runners after three to four trials each. Try different movements (e.g., skipping, hopping, moving like an animal).

STOPPING AND STARTING

Participants: Three or more.

PLAY AREA: Open green space with irregular, natural or player-made boundaries.

DESCRIPTION: One or two of the players are catchers and wear or carry an identifying object (e.g., a colour pinned to their shirt, a coloured soft ball). The remaining players are the runners. If the runners get tagged by a catchers hand or object, they must stop and perform a fun and exciting exercise of their choice and agreed upon number of reps (e.g., 10 jumping jacks, 10 mountain climbers, 10 two-foot hops). They may run again after they are touched by a free runner and told "Go."

VARIATION: This tag game plays best when the number of catchers is large enough that they succeed in tagging all of the other players. Every free runner should take part in freeing as many tagged players as they can.

A variety of games keep interest high without too much repetition. Come back to a game in a few months or reserve a few games for various seasons of the year or when a number of families are together. Play the games that are fun with larger numbers and the smaller shorter games when perhaps your own family gets to play.

More Active Games

CAPTURE THE FLAG

You'll need two flags (e.g., old towels, T-shirts, coloured material), two hoola hoops and at least eight or more participants. Each team can wear something distinctive to be recognized as a team. If different colours are worn by each team then they are more distinct, but if colours are not worn then the spy factor becomes very interesting.

Choose an open area, define boundaries (rectangular area), a centre line and an area the size of a hockey goal to be the jail.

This is a game of teamwork and strategy. Each team places a flag inside their hoola hoop. The object of the game is to steal the other team's flag and bring it back to your own side without being tagged. At the same time, you have to defend your own team's flag. If you are tagged before you reach the centre line you are taken to jail. Once the flag has been stolen from its hoop, it may only be passed laterally, if passed at all. This means it cannot be thrown to a teammate, only passed or handed off.

The only way out of jail is for one of your teammates to join hands with you to form a King's Cross (cross your arms and join hands with the crossed arms of another teammate). They must go back over the centre line in a King's Cross and then they can re-join the game.

Be ready for lots of walking and running, stopping and starting and changing directions and a lot of decision making and strategies forming.

FOUR GOAL SOCCER

This game is suitable for ages 6 and up. It requires four soccer balls, four soccer goals made with pylons, goal markings, two trees or anything you can think of to make up the goals. It can be played with any number of players. If you have fewer players, play in a smaller area, if you have many, then open up the play area. Smaller sided games are better because each player will have many more opportunities to touch the balls.

Determine the boundaries and divide the group into two teams. Each group is assigned two goals. There are no goalies. Start all four balls in the centre and choose two players to kick them out. After that, there are no other rules other than safety (no body contact). Keep score if you want. There are no designated positions. This game usually involves high participation and long endurance with lots of movement with and without a ball.

FAMILY

This game is suitable for ages eight and up. No equipment is necessary. Minimum of six or more players. Everyone sits in a circle and is numbered consecutively. Choose one player to be IT. IT calls out two more numbers. The players with those numbers must jump up and exchange seats, at the same time, IT tries to get one of the seats.

However IT can also call "family" which means everyone changes places and IT tries to sit in an empty seat. If IT succeeds in getting a seat, that person gets a turn to be IT and the game continues until everyone has had a turn or everyone tires out!

BUMP AND SCOOT

This game is suitable for ages 10 and up. It requires a volleyball-like net set up and one beach ball or other suitable large colourful and softer game ball. The game is played like volleyball. Start the game with a serve over the net. The serve can be helped over the net as necessary. Whenever a player hits the ball over the net, they "scoot" under the net to the other side. The strategy of the game is to completely switch the teams to the opposite side. The only way this can be successful is if everyone plays together. When everyone has switched sides, the game ends, or continues to "scoot" for it again.

JUGGLING GAMES

Juggling scarves, plastic grocery bags, used dryer sheets, balls or any other fun objects may be just the warm-up activity your family is looking for prior to going out for your next walk or run. To encourage everyone to be actively juggling, give them a choice of the object they want to juggle (e.g., lighter objects allow for more time to "juggle" or catch and throw that object).

- **Start with throwing and catching with one hand. Don't forget to throw as high as you can. Try about five throws.**

- **Throw and catch with the other hand. Juggling requires us to throw and catch with both hands and uses the right and left sides of our thinking brain while engaged in the activity.**

- **Try throwing with one hand and catching with the opposite. Repeat a few times switching throwing and catching hands.**

- **Try doing a turn in between each throw. Repeat a few times turning in each direction.**

- **Add one more object to juggle with, so you have two.**

- **Throw and catch each object in each hand. Repeat a few times**

- **Throw each object across your body and catch that object with the opposite hand. Repeat a few times.**

- **It's okay to talk yourself through with verbal cues: throw, throw, catch, catch...**

- **Add a third object. Try to work out a pattern. Two objects in one hand and just one in the other. *Tip: the hand with two objects has to throw first. Work on your pattern.***

- **Try juggling with a family partner. Start facing each other about one metre apart and with one object to throw and catch between the two of you. One person starts by throwing to the other; partner catches; switches hands and throws the object back. Remember, after each catch, switch hands for the throw back. Repeat a few times, and then switch directions.**

- **Add in a second object and catch and throw a few times. Work out a pattern. Add in a third, fourth and fifth object!**

- **Try a whole family juggle with a number of objects. Form a circle, with at least five family members and friends. Develop a pattern so that everyone is included, and keep an object going across the circle, not to the person beside you. Keep the object going, always throwing and catching from the same person. When ready, add in a second object, then a third, then a fourth, and yes a fifth or more!**

I guarantee you'll be ready for your family walk or run after this juggling warm-up.

Oldies but Goodies

Follow the leader, crab soccer, red light green light, hop scotch, Simon says, hide and go seek, kick the can and balloon badminton may just be the walk/run based outdoor games that you and your active family can invite others to enjoy with yourselves. Younger moms and dads, ask your own parents or grandparents and think back to your own active childhood days of playing your favourite backyard, street, field or tarmac games. They were fun, everyone was active and the games were timeless, going on for hours every play day.

A few resources to help you bring back these games:

Tossinggames.com—the world's largest tossing games forum for horseshoes to bean bags and more.

10 Fun, Wild DIY Backyard Games, from Popularmechanics.com. It has rules for kanjam, straightjacket softball and crazy croquet.

Play! Seven Backyard Games and Activities, from the Kaboose website (health.kaboose.com), provides scavenger hunts to mini Olympics ideas.

Tag, Toss, and Run: 40 Classic Lawn Games by Paul Tukey and Victoria Rowell, Story Publishers.

When inviting someone out to play, we all know how important it is to be inclusive to all members in our communities. The All Abilities web site (www.allabilitieswelcome.ca) includes a few reminders as adaptations for inclusive play:

- lighter, softer, colourful balls
- shorter, lighter striking implements
- rolling a ball instead of throwing
- striking a ball with a hockey stick rather than kicking
- increasing the number of trials or chances
- using a smaller play area
- lowering or repositioning a target

Creative Playground Playout

Take turns cheering each other through theses stations or have everyone participate together, ending each station with a loud group hug and cheer and series of high fives. Bring along water bottles for drinks after each station.

Walk, run, bike, skip, roller blade. skateboard, wheelchair your way along a safe route to the closest community park or school yard that has a creative playground (e.g., climbing, swinging, balancing structure).

Enjoy a group whole body series of stretches with everyone leading one of the stretches.

STATION 1

Planks, push-ups, front supports (support on forearms or hands and straight arms; extended body resting on both knees or with legs extended on both feet). Do them either on the ground or on a low-level cross bar that you can hold yourself in a push-up, plank or front support position. Then do as many push-ups or hold yourself in a plank or front support position for a period of time (10, 15, 20, 25 seconds or more). Start low and work your way up.

Note: Push-ups with extended legs can be successfully and safely completed only after an individual can hold themselves in a strong plank position for a period of time-strong core muscles.

STATION 2

Monkey bar hang or pull ups. Find a higher level cross bar so you can hang with feet dangling to either hold a two-arm, straight-arm hang for a few seconds or perform a few pull-ups/chin-ups for a specific time period. How many can you do in 10, 20, 30 seconds?

STATION 3

Step-ups or hop-ups on a park bench or low-level beam. Perform single leg step-ups or two-foot hops up and down for a period of time or goal setting number.

STATION 4

Kangaroo bench dips. Use the same bench or low beam. Support yourself with both hands in a rear support position, reverse push-up position. Slowly try to lower yourself from straight arms to bent arms, not too low, for a period of time or agreed upon number of kangaroo dips.

STATION 5

Sandy-side lunges. Everyone in a sandy area to perform a number of sandy-side lunges across the sandy area. Step one leg to the side then bring the other together moving across the sandy area. When you get to the end stop and lunge in the direction you just came from. Sing your favourite song as you step across the sand. Any favourite desert songs?

STATION 6

V-sit abdominal challenge. Sit in the sand or grass area and try to perform a V-sit by first holding one leg up, alternate to the other; hold up both; hold up both legs and both arms. Count to five each time.

STATION 7

Gorilla hanging V-sit challenge. Find a higher cross bar. Hold on with both hands with straight arms and legs and try to bring your knees to your waist or keep your legs straight and bring them up together into a V-sit position. Try to do as many as you can.

STATION 8

Friendly snake crawl. Find five different places on the creative playground to go over, under, slide down or crawl along. Play follow the leader as you find those safe and interesting places taking turns leading after each place has been found.

STATION 9

Create a station on your own. Have a family member volunteer a new or their favourite activity to finish with.

STATION 10

All together, shout a loud cheer!

Then walk, run, bike, skip, roller blade, skate, wheelchair your way home for a healthy snack and drink.

Play Tips for Active Children

Marjorie O'Connor, of Fit International, Edmonton, Alberta, Canada, offers these play ideas for children ages two to seven.

Children enjoy crawling over, under and around anything. They enjoy jumping, skipping, hopping and running. Try to emphasize FUN games and activities. Physical fitness activities should not be highly disciplined, structured or competitive. Children love equipment, toys and play. Use music and keep movement simple and silly. Clapping, snapping and easy movement patterns with a steady beat works well. try some hip-hop even if you don't have any hip in your hop! Children are very forgiving. Running on the spot, hopping, skipping, twisting, jumping jacks, heel jacks, knee kicks, strides and kicks are fun for them. Movement can mimic sport related activities such as skipping, bouncing balls, passing, throwing and shadow boxing.

CIRCUIT CIRCUS

Set up a mini circuit or obstacle course. Using a little innovation and any available equipment, organize a series of 5 to 10 stations: jumping jacks, hopping on a bench; jumping in and out of a hoop; throw balls into a bucket; bent knee push ups; hula hooping; rope skipping; dribbling a ball; bean bag toss; climbing a set of stairs; only to name a few; create a few more on your own.

FITNESS PARTY GAME

Try a fitness Simon says game. It works well with one child or 20. Stand in a circle and introduce movements to the children like marching, jumping jacks, running in the spot, touching toes, race walking and wiggling. The children take turns being Simon. which assists with their own creativity.

FOR PRE-TEEN AND TEENS AGES 8 TO 16 YEARS.

Create an upbeat and fun play environment. Your attitude will be a key factor in the success of your teen's fitness. Be positive and sincere. Marjorie emphasizes the 3 Zs with this age group. Keep it Zippy, no sitting around time. Be a bit Zany with the children and allow for an organized but a Zoo like environment.

Focus on the hottest trends, dance themes, extreme sports, skate board conditioning and add a touch of yoga, Pilates or tai chi for a mind, body experience. Her Boot and Body Camp class works well with teens. She incorporates an athletic style program with high performance training techniques for the Boot component and the Body is a guided stretch and relaxation series for stress reduction. Teens also enjoy a variety of circuits or fitness stations and this is a great age to introduce resistance exercises with stretch or dyna bands.

Fun Resistance Exercise Play

Resistance or strength exercise for children, youth, adults and seniors is recommended in the Canadian Physical Activity Guidelines. For children and youth and those adults just starting out using one's own body weight (e.g., push-ups, dips) is an excellent choice as well as use of stretch or dyna band resistive fitness bands. These bands are not weight bearing on joints like free weights and are available in many different resistance levels according to colour of the band. To assist with the proper colour choice for the band, the exercise should be difficult but attainable during the 9th and 10th repetition. If the exercise is easy through all 10 reps, then you are ready to progress to a stronger resistance and if the exercise is difficult at the fourth or fifth resistance, then use a lighter level band.

THE FOUR COLOUR-CODED RESISTANCE LEVELS

- **pink: light resistance**
- **green: medium resistance**
- **purple: heavy resistance**
- **silver: extra heavy resistance**

Initially, for safe and proper use guide your children through the exercise routines and start with the pink bands and progress as necessary. These bands are also excellent for bringing along on walks and runs and stopping every so often and performing a resistance exercise for a few reps or time period and then continuing with your walk or run.

Marjorie O'Connor shares this home exercise routine for the use of stretch or dyna bands.

CHEST *(Horizontal chest press)*

Put band on back across shoulder blades. Take up slack in the band. Press/straighten arms forward. *Reps: 12-15 Sets: 2*

(Wall push-ups)

Hands on wall should be slightly wider than shoulder width. Feet comfortable distance away. *Reps: 12-15 Sets: 2*

BACK *(Seated row)*

Band should be placed at the balls of the feet, lead with elbows, keep elbows close to body (elbows in). *Reps: 12-15 Sets: 2*

ABDUCTORS *(Side Step)*

Watch hips stay even, don't dip to side (tie band around both ankles) *Reps: 12-15 Sets: 2*

SHOULDERS *(Lateral raise, anterior raise- no resistance)*

Be sure to keep scapula retracted and shoulders depressed. *Reps: 12-15 Sets: 2*

BICEP *(Bicep curl)*

Stand on end of band; hold other end; elbow close to body; palm up and curl arm; keep wrist straight. *Reps: 12-15 Sets: 2*

TRICEP *(Vertical tricep press)*

Hold the middle of the band with arm across your body; grab band with working hand and extend the arm. *Reps: 12-15 Sets: 2*

LEGS *(Squats)*

Be sure to lead with the hips. Bend knees as if sitting in a chair. Perhaps practice with a chair behind you. Knees do not come over the toes. *Reps: 12-15 Sets: 2*

FOR ALL EXERCISES WHEN YOU ARE STANDING BE SURE:

- feet are shoulder width apart
- knees have slight bend in them
- back is straight
- head is straight
- shoulders are back, not elevated
- abdominals are tight (hips should be beneath you, don't tilt and create an arch in the lower back)

Quick Fun Fit Ideas

Marjorie O'Connor, is someone that we consider a fitness mentor and we go to for enjoyable and safe research-based fitness information for children, youth and adults. As Marjorie has said to us, "Keeping the fitness commitment is one step in the pursuit of achieving holistic balance and optimum health. Holistic health is the focus in the fitness world, in the health-care industry and in the physical education and health curricula. Move more, eat less and have a good time." Marjorie shares these 10-minute ideas for children, youth and adults.

10-MINUTE QUICK FUN FIT

1. CARDIO STATION

Walk, run or march on the spot for one minute. Do 10 jumping jacks and finish with one more minute of running, walking or marching on the spot.

2. STRENGTH STATION—SQUATS

Stand with your legs approximately shoulder-width apart, knees and feet facing forward. Slowly lower your body like you are going to sit down on a chair. Attempt to initiate movement from your hips. Knees should not go forward beyond your shoelaces. Return to standing position. Try 15 to 30 reps. Increase or decrease depending on your ability and fitness level.

3. CARDIO STATION

Step up on the bottom step of stairs or a solid bench for one to two minutes. Note: the platform you use should not be higher than 10 inches.

4. STRENGTH STATION—INCLINE PUSH-UPS

Using the edge of the stair, desk or elevated bench, do bent knee push-ups. For advanced, try full push-ups. Place hands on edge of bench or floor. Aim to maintain a straight back and contract abdominal muscles. Do as many as you can in one minute.

5. CARDIO STATION

Walk or run a flight of stairs for one to two minutes or do step-ups on a low bench or first step of the stairs.

6. STRENGTH STATION— MODIFIED LUNGE FROM A STANDING POSITION

Step forward and plant your foot in front of you so your knee is directly over your heel. Slowly rise, keeping your torso contracted and back straight. Now lower your body as far as you can without the left knee contacting the round. Try 8 to 15 reps. Change legs.

7. CARDIO STATION

Skipping on the spot for one to two minutes with or without a rope.

8. STRENGTH STATION— TRICEP DIPS

Sit on a sturdy chair or table. Place hands on the chair, close to the hips. Move your butt away from the edge and slowly lower body weight. Bend your elbows as you lower. Push yourself up, using your triceps (muscle on the back of your arms). These are tough. Attempt eight reps and increase when ready.

9. STRENGTH STATION—BACK EXTENSIONS

On all fours or lying face down on the floor. Slowly raise one arm and the opposite leg until they are slightly above the horizontal plane of your back. Keep movement slow and controlled. Hold for 10 seconds and change sides.

Walk/Run Map Reading Challenge

Have your active children draw a map of their backyard, nearby field or park. Materials may include computer use, or simply a pencil and paper creation. Make a running course around the area and mark it on the drawing, including easily recognizable landmarks. Map out a variety of routes. Using a coloured marker, draw a walk/run path on each map. You may want to laminate or cover the maps with plastic wrap for protection against the weather elements or sweaty hands. Go out as a group or in buddy pairs. Review the map with your children and their friends, then away they go. If several maps are made, the groups could walk/run a variety of routes.

You may consider making a map with landmarks and no designated route outlined or a map with the route marked and the children could fill in the landmarks. An alternative would be to give each active child a coded map with lines indicating different movements to be performed. For example, a straight line for walk/run, broken line for skipping and a wavy line for galloping or just write the movement at different locations on the map. Name the different areas on the map with animal names. As your active children move through that area, they must move like the animal that lives there. You might even set up stations at various locations where everyone could perform an exercise (e.g., five jumping jacks, six tuck jumps.)

There is no limit to ideas for families to have fun filled activity incorporated into their daily living.

Rainy-Day Activities

This game is suitable for ages eight and up. No equipment is necessary. Minimum of six or more players. Everyone sits in a circle and is numbered consecutively. Choose one player to be It. It calls out two more numbers. The players with those numbers must jump up and exchange seats, at the same time, It tries to get one of the seats. However It can also call "family" which means everyone changes places and It tries to sit in an empty seat. If It succeeds in getting a seat, that person gets a turn to be It and the game continues until everyone has had a turn or everyone tires out!

Here's a list of more ideas for active fun to have indoors:

- Create an indoor exercise circuit: walk up and down a set of stairs; march around the house; push-ups in the living room; crunches in a bedroom; jumping jacks in the kitchen.

- Designate an open space where everyone can roll, climb, jump, dance and tumble.

- Garages without cars can become an activity zone, even in apartments.

- Paper skate with pieces of paper under each foot.

- Mirror, mirror on the wall: copy or mirror movements by another family member or friend.

- Build an indoor obstacle course.

- Indoor hopscotch: using masking tape, outline the boxes or other creative hopscotch shapes on a floor.

- Create and play a home bowling game.

- Go on a family sightseeing adventure to an indoor leisure centre, museum, library or science centre.

Chapter 7
Nutrition

Celebration of Healthy Food

Celebrate your healthy only food choices from your own garden, nearby farmer's fields, or local markets. Plan for healthy meals, including local foods, plant your own indoor or outdoor garden, purchase healthy foods that are grown in your area, province or other parts of Canada and prepare and enjoy meals and snacks with a variety of veggies and fruits each and every day.

Planning weekly family homemade menus is a start to healthy eating. Many cost savings can be realized due to cutting out fast food purchases and heavily processed ready-to-eat meals, which contain high amounts of salts, sugars, preservatives and calories.

Canada's Food Guide provides the following ideas for healthy nutrition:

- Enjoy three meals and two to three snacks each day.
- Include all four food groups: veggies and fruits, whole grain products, milk and alternatives, and meats and alternatives.
- Enjoy three to four food groups with each meal and two to three food groups for snacks.
- Choose high-fibre foods most often: veggies, fruits and whole grains.
- Limit foods high in fat, sugar and salt.
- Make a grocery list based on your menu (and stick to it).
- Save your menus in a binder or electronic file to reuse and share.

Make healthy food choices visible in your home and community. Plant your own garden. The size can vary with your needs and available space. Gardens can be in the ground, pots or other types of planters. Community gardens are springing up in many locations. Can this be planned for and implemented in your neighbourhood? Seek permission from your local community department to open up an unused lot or space for a community garden. Having open spaces used appropriately as green gardens is better than abandoned and unkempt. This is also a great way to meet, renew, and share ideas with friends and neighbours. Families coming together to plant healthy food choices is an ideal community situation. Communities are so culturally diverse these days, community gardens are excellent for learning about herbs, spices and veggies that are new to your own food choices.Get to know your food choices. Make healthy eating a family and community affair. Together, learn about where your food comes from. Involve the whole family in meal planning, gardening and grocery shopping. Enjoy your daily physical activity through gardening by planting it, growing it and eating it.

Healthy Family Lunches

Ever wonder how many weekday lunches it takes to feed a family of four? More than one thousand per year. The encouraging news is that packing your own lunch instead of eating out or in a school cafeteria is a positive step towards reaching healthy weights for all family members. Once again, if parents or other care givers eat fruit and veggies, your children will as well. Research has shown that children eat healthier meals when the family gathers around their own table for meals. Set the example and every family member wins.

What comprises a healthy lunch? At least one fruit and two vegetables, a milk product, especially milk itself for children, a high protein food (meat or alternative or cheese), and a grain product, preferably whole grain and nutritious snacks. Enjoy a healthy family walk and talk on each person's favourite foods in each of the four food groups. Get your children involved in making their lunches, and they will be sure to eat them.

Cook ahead larger batches and freeze lunch-size portions.

For more tips and clear, practical, nutrition information you can trust, visit, **www.dieticians.ca/eatwell.** Use these interactive sites for their **Eatracker.ca**, Let's Make a Meal, Healthy Eating is in Store for You and Nutrition Challenges. learn about healthy eating for preschoolers at **www.dieticians.ca/healthystart** and initiatives in schools across Canada at **www.dieticians.ca/child**. *Canada's Food Guide* can be found at **www.hc-sc.gc.ca**. It has many healthy choices included in a variety of languages.

Get to know your food choices. Make healthy eating a family and community affair. Together, learn about where your food comes from. Involve the whole family in meal planning, gardening and grocery shopping. Enjoy your daily physical activity through gardening by planting it, growing it and eating it.

For tips and clear, practical, nutrition information you can trust visit

www.dieticians.ca/eatwell for interactive resources like eaTracker (**www.eaTracker.ca)**, Let's Make a Meal, Healthy Eating Is in Store for You, and Nutrition Challenges. Learn about healthy eating for preschoolers at **www.dieticians.ca/healthystart** and about initiatives in schools across Canada at **www.dieticians.ca/child.**

PACK HEALTHY FOODS

Poor nutrition is a concern for children. A poor diet can affect your child's learning, concentration and energy levels and may be one of the causes of childhood obesity. No one eats perfectly all of the time, but if we make it a priority for our children to eat healthy lunches, they will.

What is a healthy diet? A healthy lunch should include at least three of the four food groups. A healthy snack should include two food groups. A healthy diet for children also limits excessive salt, fat and sugar.

- **Choose whole grain products more often. Try using whole grain bread instead of white bread for sandwiches. Not all children will eat whole grain initially, try one slice of each for starters.**

- **Choose dark green and orange vegetables and orange fruit more often. Try buying one or two new choices each week to let your child discover new favourites while also adding more variety. Try serving fruits in different ways, sliced, cubed or with yoghurt for dipping. Also try lettuce, cucumber, tomato, green pepper, roasted peppers, zucchini or sweet onion slices in sandwiches.**

- **Choose lower-fat milks, cheese and yogurt in different flavours. Add natural or whole fruits to plain, low-fat yogurt.**

- **Choose leaner meats, poultry and fish, as well as dried beans, peas and lentils more often. Use lean cuts of cold, sliced meat and water-packed, canned tuna and salmon. Try some meat alternatives, such as bean chili or lentil soups.**

- **Choose other foods wisely. Pack snack foods that are high in salt, fat and sugar only occasionally, instead of daily.**

- **Encourage your child to drink plenty of water during the day.**

PLAN AHEAD

Planning takes away most of the challenges with choosing healthy foods. Healthy fun lunches get eaten when they are planned.

- **Get your child involved. If your child is included in making food choices, they are more likely to eat those choices. Your child can help plan a lunch menu and shop for groceries. Weekends are a great time to plan lunches for the coming week.**

- **Make a grocery list after the lunch menu is planned. Stick to your list at the grocery store. When you come home from the store, prepare foods so they are ready to be packed (e.g., cut and wash fruit and veggies, grate cheese).**

- **Realize how much your child can eat. Often, younger children have smaller appetites and cannot finish all the food** that is given for lunch. Pack smaller portions (e.g., a smaller piece of fruit) for younger children.

- Be organized by keeping all the necessary supplies for lunches in a convenient spot (e.g., reusable containers, lunch bags and thermos containers).

- Make lunches the night before. Younger children can assist until they are ready to pack their own healthy lunches.

BUDGETING TIPS

- Use reusable containers.
- It is less expensive to buy frozen concentrated juice than to buy the little juice boxes. (Any single portion is going to be more expensive than larger servings where you portion it out into single servings.)

- Buy foods in bulk when they are on sale (e.g., breads can be frozen).

- Purchase less "ready to eat" foods that are usually more expensive and are often higher in salt, sugar and fats (e.g., lunchmeat kits).

- Be aware of spending on less nutritious foods like fruit gummies, chips, pop and pastries. These food items offer little nutrition and should be served least often.

FOOD SAFETY

- Encourage your children to wash their hands before and after meals and snacks.
- Wash and sanitize reusable lunch containers daily.

- Always wash all fruits and vegetables before packing.

- Use an insulated lunch box with freezer packs or frozen drink containers to keep cold lunches cold.

- Refrigerate sandwiches that are made ahead of time.

- Keep hot foods hot with a thermos: fill the container with boiling water, let it stand for a few minutes, empty out the hot water and then place the hot food into the container.

With a little bit of planning throughout the year, parents can set positive examples for lifelong daily wellness choices. Eating nutritious meals and snacks together and going for a walk after supper are very simple choices that will go a long way to improving every family's health for a lifetime.

Daily Healthy Eating

As we all know, quality daily healthy eating for all family members starts with the parents or other immediate caregivers.

- Eating meals together helps to foster a healthy environment. Plan family meals and let everyone have input and assist with meal preparation.

- Eating breakfast is essential for an active and productive day performing one's daily routines.

- What foods does your family enjoy? Healthy and balanced portion sizes for everyone from the four groups, especially fruits and veggies and a little protein for each meal.

- With a little planning from everyone, a variety of natural, whole fruits, vegetable and protein sources can be affordable and convenient.

- Try a new or ethnic recipe that can be the perfect way to add spice to your nutritious life.

- Nutritious food leftovers are excellent for daily school and work lunches.

- Create a "bucket list" of healthy eating choices to try all through the year.

- The Canada Food Guide shares valuable nutrition information and is available in over 10 different languages.

Canada's Food Guide

By learning more about *Canada's Food Guide*, families will learn more about how much food each family member needs, what types of foods are better for you and the importance of physical activity in one's day. It can be viewed at **www.hc-sc.gc.ca** or **www.eatwellbeactive.gc.ca.**

HOW MUCH FOOD DO YOU NEED EVERY DAY?

How much food you require from each of the four food groups depends upon age and sex. Example: A chart includes ages 2 to 51 years plus. If you have girls or boys ages 9 to 13 they require the following: six servings of veggies and fruit, six servings of grain products, three to four servings of milk and alternatives and one to two servings of meat and alternatives.

WHAT IS A FOOD GUIDE SERVING?

A serving refers to the amount or portion size. The guide provides examples of one Food Guide serving: e.g., one cup of leafy raw vegetables or salad and one piece of fruit.

MAKING WISE CHOICES?

Provides tips for home, school, work or when eating out. For example, eat at least one dark green and one orange vegetable each day. Make at least half of your grain products whole grain each day. Drink skim, 1% or 2% milk each day. Eat at least two Food Guide servings of fish each week.

PHYSICAL ACTIVITY?

Being active every day for at 60 to 90 minutes is a step towards better health and body weight.

ENJOY EATING?

Enjoying family meal times and get togethers at home is linked to better nutrient intake and lifestyle habits in children and teenagers. Try to experience a variety of food and take the time to enjoy each bite and bit of conversation.

The Food Guide also provides tips on how to best choose from the four food groups, planning meals, shopping tips, reading food labels, fast and easy meal ideas, smart snacking, eating out and counting Food Guide servings in a meal.

Try using the Food Guide with the Dieticians of Canada eaTracker **(www.eatracker.ca)** to keep track of your daily intake. You can also make a simple refrigerator chart yourself with the following titles: Food; Food Group; No. of Servings; Day/Date. Right beside your food chart make another one for physical activity with the following titles: Name of Activity; Time; Type; How I Felt; Total Time. These charts can reflect individual or entire family information.

Food For Thought

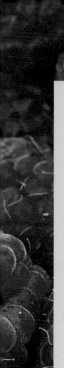

Setting goals for improving eating habits can be a very smart tool for active children and families. Start by recording everything you eat during each day. Compare the records to *Canada's Food Guide to Healthy Eating*, which is the recognized standard for healthy, balanced eating patterns by nutrition professionals and health educators. Families can see where they practise good eating habits and where they may benefit from a few changes. Active children and their families can set short-term goals to improve in one small area at a time (e.g., add one more fruit and veggie to lunch and snack choices each week).

Every family member can help each other in meeting their new goals:

- Help each other complete a one-day food record.

- Talk about the value of continuous improvement in all areas of life, including activity and nutrition.

- Set a few short- and long-term goals together. They can be both individual and family goals.

- Brainstorm ideas for healthy only eating.

- Eat at least one meal a day as a family.

- Talk about the foods everyone eats each day to perform their daily routines.

- Increase water consumption and reduce or eliminate the amount of high-sodium and sugary drinks.

- Grocery shop together as a family and discuss healthy food choices.

- Research fast-food and restaurant outlets for their nutrition information.

Take a balanced approach to your family's nutrition. Eat healthy, stay active and have fun with your "only" healthy choices.

Nutrition Tips for Active Children

Marjorie O'Connor offers a few tried and tested nutritional tips and snacking ideas to keep children happy, healthy and high in energy for play and performing their daily routines at home, school and in their communities.

1 Eat at home as a family more often than not over each week.

2 Use low-fat dairy products instead of whole milk whenever possible. But don't take it to the extreme. Children should be consuming whole milk until at least two years old. Fat is essential for children's growth and energy. Dieticians recommend that parents look at lower-fat dairy products for daily food preparation but avoid excessive use of fat-free items.

3 After ensuring your child gets all the milk they need, offer water as much as possible. Water drinking throughout the day is a great lifelong habit to get into at a young age.

4 Children love pizza. Instead of choosing toppings high in saturated fat, like pepperoni and sausage, use more veggies and skim-milk mozzarella cheese.

5 When shopping for cereals, look for the whole grain, low-sugar brands. Sugar should not be the first ingredient listed.

6 Aim to give the family more whole grain breads. They provide 65% more nutrients than refined white bread.

7 Use fruit spread on toast and skip the butter, especially if using peanut butter or other nut butters.

8 Make great burgers with lean ground round, ground chicken breast or ground white turkey meat. Also veggie and tofu burgers have come a long way over the years. They are low in fat, high in nutrients and taste good.

9 Pretzels, unlike potato chips, contain only a trace of fat. Use unsalted or whole wheat, if possible. Air-popped popcorn tastes great with parmesan cheese or other toppings available at many bulk food sections.

10 A fun and tasty fruit kabob can be made with slices of kiwi, banana, apple and strawberries on a skewer. Dip in orange juice and roll in unsweetened coconut.

11 Veggies with dip are terrific. How about making carrot coins for dunking? Ants in a log can be made with celery filled with cheese spread or peanut butter and sprinkled raisins.

12 Freeze grapes, bananas, blueberries, pineapple or melon chunks for a healthful snack. Instead of buying popsicles or Slurpees, try crushing ice and top with unsweetened fruit juice.

13 Beans and lentils contain protein with no cholesterol or fat and lots of fibre. Sneak them into meatloaf, salads and sauces.

14 Switch from ice cream bars to fruit and juice bars, frozen yogurt, skim milk fudge bars, fruit sorbet and ice milk.

15 For your little cookie monsters try Animal Crackers, Fig Newtons, ginger snaps, baby cookies and vanilla wafers. They contain sugar but are lower fat choices.

Family Nutrition

Millions of books are dedicated to the topics of nutrition and weight control. A single chapter can only brush the surface of our understanding of nutrition. Here are some ideas that should help provide you with appropriate guidelines to make healthy eating part of an active family lifestyle.

A major issue facing most families is how to make better choices in your daily intake of food and liquids. Think of one glass of water filled with our daily intake of calories and another glass filled with your daily output of calories through exercise and daily living. If you or your child is at the perfect weight and body fat content, then you will strive to have the same amounts of water in both glasses. For the vast majority of us trying to lose a few pounds, however, the goal is to have a larger glass for the output than for the input. This idea is really fundamental to successful family meal and activity planning.

Many people become obsessed with the fat and oil contents of their food while neglecting to take note of the total number of calories consumed. Too many calories taken in, even from healthy foods such as salads, breads and lean meats, still get converted to fat for storage, which is why family exercise is so vital. The most important thing is a balance between the amount of exercise your family gets and the amount of food you consume. What we choose to eat is what can really give us an advantage in weight management. More importantly, we must think of our total well-being rather than just management of our body weight. And the key to family success is getting everyone to think about the balance of nutrition and exercise.

Healthy Eating Choices

Activity can challenge your body beyond what you thought possible. The human body undergoes a multitude of very positive physical changes in response to training. Blood volume expands to allow greater amounts of oxygen to reach body cells, muscle mass increases and the body becomes adept at storing the fuel that will carry it to the end of the race or other athletic event. These changes allow you to finish your target event strong and upbeat. However, significant work is required on your part if you hope to reap these benefits. Consistent training, eating healthily and sleeping enough are all needed to lay the foundation that will support you during your activity and the activity of family life.

The good news is that crafting an active family's well-balanced diet is enjoyable and easy to do, provided you keep a few basic principles in mind.

Photo credit: Wong Mei Teng

SPORTS NUTRITION BASICS

Your active family members are athletes in the truest sense of the word. Frequent activities of a longer duration increase your nutrient requirements. Responding to these heightened needs helps you maximize your enjoyment and strengthen your performance.

CALORIES COUNT

Balance, variety and moderation are the keys to a responsible nutritional plan—no one food or food group is over- or underemphasized. In practical terms, a healthy active diet

- **provides abundant amounts of wholegrain products, vegetables and fruit**
- **contains moderate amounts of protein and fat**
- **limits (not eliminates) less nutritious foods, such as margarine, butter, higher-fat snack foods, sweets, sodas and fruit juices**

When families eat is very important as well. A regular, consistent eating pattern is essential in terms of helping young athletes meet their caloric needs. Kids need to eat at least three meals and three or four snacks each day to match the energy that they expend during their times of activities. Infrequent eating, skipping meals and chronic dieting can make getting enough calories very difficult. Avoiding these practices will enhance performance and allow you to make the most of your athletic events.

CARBOHYDRATES

Carbohydrate is an essential nutrient that serves as the body's prime source of fuel during physical activity. In addition, carbohydrate is essential for using or "burning" fat as a source of energy. Without adequate amounts of carbohydrate, your body will be unable to draw on your fat stores to fuel your activity.

In foods, carbohydrates are found in two forms: simple carbohydrates (sugars) and complex carbohydrates (starches). In the body, both forms are digested or broken down to make glucose, the sugar that fuels all of our cells. During activity, glucose circulating in our blood can be withdrawn for use as an immediate source of fuel. Athletes can also store glucose in their muscles and liver in a complex form called glycogen. Glycogen functions much like a back-up or reserve fuel tank on a truck or motorcycle. During prolonged activity, the body can dip into its glycogen "tank," or stores, for an added source of glucose.

Adequate carbohydrate intake is essential. When carbohydrate intake is marginal, glycogen is not stored in the amounts needed to support being active for more than an hour. As a result, endurance drops dramatically in those who do not take in enough carbohydrate. This phenomenon can end even the best-trained athlete's dreams of success. Depleting your glycogen stores has the same effect as a car running out of gas—things come to a halt. You cannot rebuild your glycogen stores during a long run or training session. Recognizing this, it's critically important that you take in enough carbohydrate on a daily basis. At least 55% to 65% of the energy (calories) should come from this nutrient. Translated into food, this is a diet that contains approximately 5 to 12 servings of grain products, where one serving equals:

- 1 slice of bread
- 30 g of cold cereal
- 175 mL (¾ cup) hot cereal
- ½ bagel, pita or bun
- 125 mL (½ cup) cooked pasta or rice

Plus 5 to 10 servings of vegetables and fruit, where one serving equals:

- 1 medium-sized vegetable or fruit
- 125 mL (½ cup) fresh, frozen, or canned vegetables or fruit
- 250 mL (1 cup) salad
- 125 mL (½ cup) vegetable or fruit juice

WATER—CHOICE OF CHAMPIONS

About two-thirds of the human body is made up of water. The best way to rehydrate is with water. Fruit juices, sodas, sports drinks and flavoured mineral waters all come with added sugars. A canned soft drink can contain as much as 12 teaspoons of sugar! A 250 mL glass of apple juice can contain the equivalent of six teaspoons of sugar. Water is still the best choice for champions young and old. For children above two years, milk is a great source of hydration and a great source of calcium, important for bone and teeth development.

Get everyone in your family packing a water bottle with them wherever they go and encourage them to drink frequently. In a summer lunch or snack bag, pack a frozen bottle of water. Keep cold water in your home rather than sweet drinks—encourage your kids to drink water rather than sports drinks or add a few slices of lemon, orange or mint to your jug of cold water. Drink water and eat fresh fruit rather than drinking fruit juices.

Water helps your body keep your temperature stable, carries nutrients and oxygen to cells, cushions joints, protects organs and tissues, and removes wastes. You lose water from your sweating, breathing and peeing.

Some general guidelines for daily water intake

Age	Male	Female
9 - 13	6 Glasses	5 Glasses
14 - 18	7 Glasses	6 Glasses
Adults	10 Glasses	8 Glasses

Headaches, fatigue, crankiness, and poor concentration and co-ordination are signs of dehydration.

Active muscles generate heat and fluids help in the removal of heat. Exercising in the heat poses unique problems for kids. They sweat less than adults, so they have a great heat gain in hot weather. On hotter days, kids should be drinking every 10 to 15 minutes and be encouraged to pour water over themselves to help keep cool.

PRE-ACTIVITY EATING

"What should I eat before a run or event?" is a common question and one that can haunt you if you have incorrect information. Eating at the wrong time or choosing the wrong kind of foods can produce symptoms like nausea, vomiting and diarrhea—experiences that rarely make for a fun run!

Eating before activity, or pre-event eating as sport nutritionists refer it to, serves some very important purposes. A sound pre-event meal or snack can

- **enhance endurance**
- **prevent hunger and dehydration**
- **promote mental alertness**

Different people tolerate eating before activity differently. Experimentation is important for finding the exact combination of foods that works best for you.

Timing is critical in terms of pre-event eating. Foods need time to be digested in order to serve as a source of energy. Recognizing this fact, it's important to allow time between a moderately sized meal and the start of an activity. Smaller snacks can be consumed a little closer to the start of a run or activity.

A nutritious snack, eaten just before bed, helps to keep blood glucose levels stable. This approach, coupled with a very light snack in the hour prior to a activity, may help you sneak in a bit more sleep before you start an early morning family bike or hike

Foods rich in complex carbohydrates, such as breads, pasta, cereals or grains, are broken down quickly to provide the body with a source of glucose and are ideal choices before exercise. Fluids help to hydrate the body and should be part of all pre-event meals.

Many people have difficulty tolerating the following kinds of foods, which should be eaten with caution before activity:

- **high-sugar foods: honey, regular soft drinks, syrups, candy and table sugars. These foods can cause abdominal cramping and diarrhea.**

- **high-fibre foods: bran cereals and muffins, legumes (e.g., beans, peas, lentils), and raw vegetables. High-fibre foods can produce bloating, gas and diarrhea.**

- **high-fat or high-protein foods: butter, margarine, salad dressings, peanut butter, hamburger, hot dogs, etc. Fat and protein take longer to digest than carbohydrates and are not a good source of quick fuel during exercise.**

Examples: Pre-activity Meals and Snacks

Breakfast
250 mL (1 cup) Rice Krispies
250 mL (1 cup) skim milk
1 banana
250 to 500 mL (1 to 2 cups) plain, cool water

Snack
1 cinnamon-raisin bagel
½ banana or apple
250 mL (1 cup) low-fat yogurt
125 mL (½ cup) strawberries

Family Weight Management

What works for family weight management?

To look at the plethora of magazine articles, books and websites, you might think that there isn't anything that works as far as long-term weight management is concerned. In fact, just the opposite is true. Registered dietitians and nutrition researchers have a very clear picture of the approaches that best support weight loss, as well as those that don't: *(continued on next page)*

- Begin by rethinking your focus. View weight loss as one small part of a larger plan to "retrain" your overall lifestyle. Focus on developing healthy eating habits rather than dieting restrictively to drop a few pounds quickly. Remind yourself that learning new habits is difficult, and expect to experience periods of frustration along the way.

- Be realistic. Aim for a goal weight that is ideal for the individual. A realistic goal weight is one that you can maintain without resorting to constant dieting or extreme exercise programs. It is a weight that allows you to fully enjoy the activities of daily life and that gives you a sense of well-being.

- Keep moving! Exercise plays a critical role in weight loss and long-term weight maintenance. Traditional weight loss diets frequently ignore the important link between exercise and weight maintenance. Without regular exercise, dieters tend to lose some muscle tissue along with any body fat that is lost. Loss of muscle tissue tends to slow metabolism (the rate that you burn calories). As a result, inactive dieters are much more likely to regain any weight that they have lost when they abandon their diet and return to a less restrictive way of eating. Regular exercise can help to prevent this situation from occurring.

- Focus on eating for health instead of dieting. Traditional weight loss diets are often nutritionally imbalanced, overly restrictive and woefully unsuccessful. As a result, most people cannot stick with this kind of eating pattern long-term, and achieving a healthy weight becomes impossible. Aim for a nutrient-rich eating style—based on *Canada's Food Guide*—that is low enough in calories to promote gradual, healthy weight loss.

- Opt for small changes instead of a complete lifestyle "renovation." Changing behaviour takes work, and building new eating habits or creating an active lifestyle are no exceptions. However, you can make things much easier if you phase in change slowly over time. Research shows that people adapt best to small changes rather than complete lifestyle "renovations." Recognizing this, don't aim to change your eating habits overnight. Focus on revamping one meal or one food choice at a time, letting yourself become comfortable with your new approach before adding anything new.

Keep up the fluids! Continuing to take in plenty of fluids after exercise helps to combat dehydration by replacing water that was lost from your body during exercise.

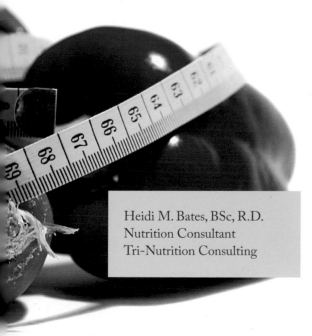

Heidi M. Bates, BSc, R.D.
Nutrition Consultant
Tri-Nutrition Consulting

Chapter 8
Strategies for Success

Daily Physical Activity and Nutrition Bins

One of the more successful strategies to promote daily physical activity in schools across Canada is providing daily physical activity bins in each classroom. They are filled with age-appropriate equipment for students to use at various times through the day. How about a similar bin for your home?

All you need is a large plastic tote container or large hockey-type bag placed in a high-traffic area or other suitable location in your house. Have everyone contribute to the play loot in the bin. There should be one or two special items for everyone. Here are a few ideas: marbles, skipping rope, hacky sacks, exercise bands, various types and sizes of balls, hula hoops, play parachute material, sticks or bats. The bin doesn't have to contain expensive stuff. Look at neighbourhood garage and yard sales, where you can often find a good deal for sports-related equipment or toys.

You can also put nutrition reminders in the bin. Include a family set of named water bottles beside the bin so everyone remembers to drink lots of water during those play periods. (Don't forget to wash them every so often.) You could also include a special snack note, such as "take some fruit or healthy snack bar with you." Include a box of healthy granola bars by the bin. It's a good idea to take along healthy snacks, two to three snacks each day, especially for longer activity.

Have fun with your activity bins.

Daily Physical Activity (DPA)

- Parents and other primary caregivers are the best positive role models for children when it comes to daily play.

- Sitting less each day and moving "under your own steam" add to daily physical activity minutes. Aim for a minimum of 30 minutes each and every day.

- New technologies and learning tools should be embraced and supported. Choose educational screen time over idle screen time. Screen games such as tennis do not necessarily lead to playing the actual game outside on a tennis court.

- Playing with your children has mutual benefits. Try following your toddler around—they make excellent pace bunnies.

- Children are not miniature adult elite athletes. Include free play in addition to developmentally appropriate organized play and structured sports and activity programs.

- Your neighbourhood community is your outdoor gymnasium. Get out and have fun on the creative playground. Everyone—children of all ages, adults and seniors—can run, swing, hang, jump and balance. Play hopscotch, 4 square, tag, kick the can, double Dutch, red light/green light, Simon says, hide and go seek, throwing and catching with a variety of objects and balls, and anything else that comes to mind.

- As an active family, smile and say hello to those you meet along the way to share your joy for playing often and together.

 Be proud and loud—tell people you're an athlete. You never know whom you may inspire.

Family Talk Time

Many families try to get together for family meetings to discuss a variety of topics that help children develop socially and emotionally through their childhood and adolescent years.

Daily physical activity and daily healthy eating discussions can also occur during these family talk times. Walking and talking might be a strategy to pursue while discussing how daily physical play and healthy eating practices are very beneficial for one's body.

When you are active by moving, playing, working and exercising, you help yourself become physically fit. Share with your children how being active helps the body get better at performing basic physical skills, just as doing homework and studying helps the mind become smarter.

Talk about the many fun ways they can move, play and add more daily physical activity into their day at home and in school. Ask for examples of ways that make being active fun, such as being with a friend, pets, parents or siblings or adding music to indoor play sessions.

Perhaps you can ask your children to describe in writing their favourite ways of being active by playing and what physical fitness means to them. Post those on a refrigerator door or a high-traffic bulletin board location.

Let your children know that it's okay not to always feel physically well during or after playing very hard. Sometimes it does hurt a little and will make them feel tired. Discuss the difference between play being hard and hurting a little (e.g., breathing hard after running as fast as one can) versus activity that makes you feel very bad and seriously hurting (e.g., bruising from contact games). The body will adapt to playing hard. Some children may not feel too well if they have done too much. It is better to start slowly and progress to a more challenging routine.

Daily healthy eating habits can be discussed in terms of their energy requirements for play. Whole, unprocessed foods are better than any processed foods. Provide examples from *Canada's Food Guide* for daily servings, protein and fruit and vegetable requirements. Explain that allowing only daily healthy food choices for snacks and meals will allow everyone to play longer and better.

Have everyone keep their own journal or diary and make entries about feeling good when playing. What made them feel good? Have them describe an occasion they didn't feel well when playing. Some of their thoughts may reflect physical, social, emotional and intellectual challenges that they may require assistance with over coming.

Remember, being a healthy role model includes building healthy self esteem in your children. Gentle and positive encouragement will be more beneficial as an active family than constant pressure and negative comments.

These discussions can lead to lifelong healthy play and eating choices as the only choices so that every family member's lifestyle is the healthiest and best it can be.

Family Fan Club

It's time we gave each family member a series of well-deserved high fives for accepting and cooperating together through the challenges that your "only" healthy daily play and eating choices may be providing. As often as daily or weekly, plan some cheer time together. There is power in positive affirmation for oneself and as an entire family.

By changing the way we think and talk to ourselves and each other, we can change all kinds of things about the way we act, feel and display ourselves. Encourage each other with positive family talk. Congratulate each other for wanting to change by supporting and making those "only" choices easier and easier.

Moving More Together

Sitting too much each day can be thought of as a disease. So sitting less each day can be thought of as a cure. Parents or other primary caregivers who fill the bleachers, sidelines or other waiting areas watching their children or spouse practise and play their favourite activities, from hockey to soccer to music and dance, should get up and out for a walk or run.

You could organize a parent skate around, shinny hockey or soccer game on an adjacent sheet of ice or field. Adults can arrange to bring their ball gloves to play catch together.

I'll bet you can find an extra bat to give up a few fly balls with. Get onto the track or cross-country running trail for a walk or run while your children are practising their skills. How about an adult singing lesson, art class or dance lesson alongside or in an adjacent room.

During games and performances, a quick active walk during breaks or between periods might work. What do you think? It's a great way to get those daily activity minutes in during heavily scheduled children days.

The Active Places We Live In

Take a look around your neighbourhood, community, town or city. Many of us can share a variety of personal and family stories about making the best of the year-round locations and opportunities to be out and about being active. From personal spaces to natural and developed parks to indoor or outdoor recreation facilities, our communities play a large role in promoting participation for all age groups. Whether for fun, fitness or glory, communities offer many programs that will suit anyone and all interests from beginner to elite levels. Your communities reflect a culture choice for active and healthy living for all.

Speak up and out often about the many year-round active environments and opportunities your community has to offer, including those that you have created on your own. All family, caregivers, friends and community members are role members for each other, especially for the children and youth in your community. Share your family active story with each other, your children at school and adults at work. Sometimes we feel isolated by our actions and thoughts for healthy active lifestyles. By sharing our beliefs to a wider audience we will soon find others who understand and practise healthy nutritional and physical practices. They will provide a wonderful support network that may be missing and pull the community together for the greater good. As parents, we can at times appreciate role model support from other families in the greater community.

Appreciating the places you live in and making the best of the active opportunities your communities have to offer throughout the year will provide a natural support group for creating, planning and supporting any "missing" community active strategies for the future.

Sharing Your Active Family Story

Make it your family challenge to share all of the good things that your active family is experiencing as a result of the positive lifestyle changes you've made in your daily physical activity and nutrition choices. It doesn't matter if you are just starting to implement a few changes to your family's physical activity and nutritional choices or if your family is well on its way to a complete lifestyle change.

Let other relatives, neighbours, friends, colleagues and community members know how happy your family feels, looks, acts and behaves. It copes and performs daily routines better than ever as a result of the conscious, positive lifestyle changes you have made by including a little or a lot more daily physical activity and healthy eating choices into your daily family routines. They are now part of your daily life choices—embedded into your daily routines—and will naturally occur for the rest of your family life, forever active.

Take someone under your wing and include them in your healthy positive environment. It could be a relative, your child's school or neighbourhood friend, a family in your neighbourhood or colleague at work. Provide them with the necessary supports, which they may lack, so that they too can experience the struggles, growing pains, small successes and life-changing wellness experiences that your family went through on its journey toward personal and family healthy behaviours.

The research continues to support the importance of parental role modelling for behaviour change and participation in physical activity and healthy food choices. Young children, teens and youth who have parents who are active at least three times per week for 30 to 60 minutes per day are also active for the same amount of times per week. Parents who eat at home for the majority of their meals and snacks will pass those healthy habits on to their children more times than not.

We know and are experiencing the overall benefits of daily physical activity and healthy food choices as individuals and families. It's not just for weight loss and the societal ideal body shape or weight as reflected in mass media. Healthy, lifelong physical activity behaviours for all ages, especially for children and youth, "allow children to enjoy physical activity, exercise, sport and free play just because they are intrinsically enjoyable pursuits. The ultimate goal should be to facilitate the development of an intrinsic understanding that being physically active is imperative to a healthy life that is free of chronic illness and disease." (Healthy Active Kids Canada Report Card for Children and Youth, 2008).

Families have an important role to play in modelling healthy behaviours. All daily healthy activities and eating habits are not only "good for the heart" but also "good for our hearts."

Parental Influences

Encourage your children with their daily physical activity choices, no matter which participation ability level they are at, from organized sport programs to free play choices. Get involved as a coach, volunteer, organizer or active role model (e.g., walk or run around the soccer field or indoor arena when your children are practising or playing). Encourage active opportunities during vacations, birthdays or free play occasions in your neighbourhood. Take turns with other families in making your homes the community indoor and outdoor gyms for the neighbourhood children. Give the gift of physical activity for family birthdays—give a present that encourages activity like a new pair of runners, swim suit, pedometer, ball or bicycle.

Consider a walking or wheeling, "moving under one's own steam" school bus for your neighbourhood.

This involves two or more families travelling to and from school together for activity and safety.

The benefits of active transport to and from school include:

- increased physical activity for children, teens and youth and parents

- parents can extend their walks/runs after the children are at school by taking a longer route home or including school pickup time in their 30 to 60 minute walk/run/wheel home

- visible support for healthy active family lifestyles in one's school community

- encouraging less vehicle traffic congestion around schools, leading to a healthier and cleaner environment

- building confidence and self esteem in participants by encouraging looking after one self

- a fun and social time for all neighbourhood participants that builds a sense of positive community

- positive relations developed between school and community—positive and healthy, active minds at school

Advocate with your school's parent council to ensure that all age groups in your community have access to the school facilities after school hours. Encouraging and developing strategies for affordable use of school and community facilities is a key for all actively minded communities. Are the school and community playgrounds accessible for many ages of children, teens and youth? Can our special needs children, teens, and youth go for a swing or slide or climb on the creative playgrounds?

At your first parent/teacher conference ask about the physical activity opportunities available and planned for all students.

- Is physical activity a social norm in the school?

- Does the school and district have a nutrition policy and how is it implemented in the school and classrooms?

- Are healthy food choices available?

- Can we look closely at the ingredients for those hot dog/pizza day offerings?

- Can healthy fruit kabob and veggie days be included?

Many of you already possess the skills to take up the challenge to encourage, involve yourself and facilitate necessary healthy changes in your school and community environments. However, if you are looking for support and ideas on how to get started contact your local school boards, public health agencies or provincial, state and national active living organizations. It may take time, but we know it's worth creating and visibly supporting healthy and active environments for all ages of citizens.

Active Time of Our Lives

Decide to have the "active time of our lives" this year. As experienced or new parents, you are called upon to provide many physical, social, emotional, intellectual and spiritual supports for your family. You typically reflect upon your own childhood memories with your own parents or caregivers. Did we have active or non-active childhood memories? Those non-active memories can certainly be changed into active "times of our lives."

Many of you who enjoyed active healthy childhoods have much to thank your parents for. Many of you remember coming home from school, grabbing a quick homemade snack, and then racing out the door to the street or park to start one of many games of hockey, soccer, baseball, hide and go seek or other creative, fun, made on the spot games. You usually had more than enough kids for two teams or more. Everyone played, picked captains, made the teams fair and got right into playing very quickly because it would get dark soon or you would get called in for supper.

Above all you had a great time, each and every day. You played through all seasons, slipping and sliding through the snow covered streets and fields, jumping into the community pool for hours at a time, playing a game of tag or just chasing or racing each other in a park. Leagues and games were not organized and adult supervision was minimal. Winning was important, but for everyone playing was most important. Will your children feel thankful and carry activity forward in their own lives and future families?

Healthy household habits, both indoors and out, regular physical activity and lots of healthy role modelling can set young children on the path to positive family active traditions for the "time of their lives" for many years of memories and active lifestyles. Give your children a chance to love to play, to experience the joy of playing and being naturally fit and not to be part of any childhood obesity epidemic.

Here are 10 ways to have the active time of your lives:

1 Save active time for yourself and your family. Sit less each day. Many daily routines can become active ones. Walk or run to your usual places: to the grocery store, movie store, school and work. Walk and read at a library. Walk or run to a friend's home. Walking and public transportation go hand in hand. Rather than jumping in your car, everyone jumps into their runners to get to their needed or favourite location.

2 Role modelling from caregivers is still the number one strategy for ensuring active behaviours in children. Take your role very seriously. "Doing as I say" does not go as far as "Doing as I do." Remember you are being watched by your children.

3 Break into spontaneous activity. Every so often just stand up and get active. Anyone can lead and no

planning is required. Turn on the music and dance, stretch, do yoga or go for a walk or run. Walk rather than taking the car. Just go with the active flow. Anytime is a good time. This may be the answer for a family member that is feeling down or stressed, relax and play and have a conversation about things. You'll be surprised how this will re-energize yourself and those around you.

4 Create an active "flash mob" experience. This can be done at home, in your neighbourhood or other more public spaces (e.g., mall).

5 Paying it forward, giving back, sharing your expertise. Those who are well on their way to implementing their healthy active family routines can comfortably share their strategies with other families, friends, colleagues or extended family members. Others may need help with getting started or are looking for a needed boost to their routines. Have them join your family or go to their place of residence or local park—they may never have been there before. Support each other to try a new winter activity. (Winter seems to be one of the more challenging times of the year to get outside.) Build up everyone's networking channels by phone, email, Facebook or Twitter. Share your active blogs.

6 Plan and prepare for a spring walk or run together as active families. The possibilities in most immediate and nearby communities are endless.

7 Support your active children playing an organized sport or activity. Car pooling for children and practices makes sense for many reasons. However, car pooling caregivers, moms and dads to games and practices is even more important. Attend as many games and practices or competitions as possible. Attend more than you can't. Change those personal work schedules. Watch your children kick, hit, roll, wheel, flip or dance to something they are very good at and enjoy. Remember your kids are watching, to see if you are there. They may not admit it, but they love having all of you and both of you present. Walking around the arena or field is also okay when you are out there. I'll bet your children will want to watch you participate in your own organized sport or activity.

8 Joyful play is fun. Challenging oneself with the right amount of competition will keep everyone coming back for more. That winning feeling can be felt by everyone on their walk/runs or playing an organized sport, from hockey to gymnastics. Unstructured active play time is very important at home and school, especially for your very young children. The same goes at work. Lunch walks, walking a message to a colleague, active work meetings or walking meetings all make sense.

9 Play outside more often. Children and perhaps adults need to set limits on screen time, whether computer or TV time. Do your children really need a TV in their bedrooms? Get your children out. As active adults we enjoy our trail walk/runs and all that nature has to offer. Taking your children for nature walks is the start of something very special for your children, not just from a fitness perspective but also to create an appreciation for their natural environments. They will feel more comfortable and safer with being outdoors, in parks, sports fields and natural forested areas.

10 Active family traditions. So what's it going to be? A walk after dinner; exercise breaks, morning, noon or night; weekend bike rides, from training wheels to road bikes; a walk/run to a favourite weekend restaurant, to neighbours or to grandparents' house for breakfast or lunch; burn calories going and returning. Thanksgiving day is game day for us—hockey, football, you name it. Try a Halloween neighbourhood barbecue in costumes followed by everyone walking/running for treats together through the community. Meet other families at an annual community walk/run. Visit older children at out-of-town universities/colleges/residences a distance away and coincide the visit with a community walk/run event in that community. Meet an out-of-town family member at an annual event somewhere in North America or beyond (e.g., Boston Marathon, New York Marathon). Meeting every Sunday afternoon at the community leisure centre for the community league swim and greet sessions. Everyone prepares and sits together for at least one full day of meals, breakfast, lunch, dinner and snack times.

Can you and your children add any more?

Healthy household habits, both indoors and out, regular physical activity and lots of healthy role modelling can set young children on the path to positive family active traditions for the "time of their lives" for many years of memories and active lifestyles.

Get to Know an Olympic and Paralympic Athlete

Learning about an elite athlete can be very exciting for all family members. On your family physical activity calendar, highlight the next summer and winter games. Search the Internet or walk to your local library or your children's school library to find Olympic resources. The Olympic Games are built on the ideals of sportsmanship, fair play and hard work—to do one's best demonstrating that desire and passion to participate. Sound family familiar?

At the official Olympics website **(www.olympic.org)**, you can click on the upcoming Olympic and Paralympic Games logos to find all of the particulars for each games. Go to the Canadian Olympic website **(www.olympic.ca)** where Canadian athletes are highlighted for the upcoming summer and winter games. The Canadian Olympic School Programs get you inspired with Olympic stories, activities, interviews, videos and contests. At both the Olympic and the Paralympic sites you can click on any of the individual sport logos to find more information.

As a family, make two lists of all Olympic and Paralympic Games sports. Carefully tear up your lists and place each of the sport names in two separate containers. Have each family member take turns choosing one sport from each bag to research and share and to meet a Canadian athlete competing in that sport. Schedule Olympic talk times, perhaps when you are engaged in a family warm up prior to that walk or run, for everyone to share their findings.

Send an email, tweet, blog or write a letter to a Canadian Olympic or Paralympic athlete. They would appreciate hearing from your family. Everyone can choose from the list a number of times throughout the year leading up to the games, whatever makes sense to your family. Choose an athlete from another country or one from a specific sport that you want to learn more about. As the games get closer, find out whom our Canadian athletes will be competing against.

Contact the local or provincial sporting associations to receive an introduction to a winter or summer Olympic or Paralympic sport. During Olympic years, these sports organizations are very active promoting their sports. Take a few lessons to learn cross-country skiing, biathlon, downhill skiing, luge or skeleton, how to throw a javelin or shot put, or walk/run the 10,000 metre event on a local track. What are the Paralympic sports? Why not try a few.

Being athletic you experience the thrill of crossing a finish line and having others cheer you…it's your Olympic moment.

Comprehensive Health Approach—Schools, Homes, Communities

Many schools, school districts and education and health ministries across North America have adopted comprehensive programs for the health and wellness of their students and staff. As outlined in many provincial curricula across Canada, this approach includes an emphasis on

- **health and physical education instruction that promotes a commitment to healthy choices and behaviours**

- **the coordination of health and community services that focus on health promotion and the provision of appropriate services to students and families who require assistance and interventions**

- **providing environments that promote and support behaviours that enhance the health of students, families and school personnel**

This approach helps children, youth and their families understand how they can have control over many conditions that affect their health. Parents can provide a family perspective on sensitive topics and promote supports at home for new health and physical activity information that children are learning

at school. You can be supportive of existing comprehensive school health programs or make inquiries about introducing this approach in your school.

A comprehensive approach naturally fosters partnerships through programs and activities for families, volunteers and community groups. It encourages school staff, parents and community agencies to work together to achieve shared health and wellness goals. Partnerships can be small—a few individuals working together—or large—a collective of community groups forming partnerships with entire school districts.

We have made many great strides at home and in schools with respect to healthy food and snack choices, but the corner store or fast food outlet in our community continues to provide many unhealthy choices. Can we suggest, support and create a few food choice balances in the greater community? Do you have a walkable community? Is it safe to walk or cycle to school or work? Is public transportation convenient? How can you work with your community contacts to solve some of these questions? Does your school have a nurse? Do your community health nurses only come to schools to give needles? Many school nurses are more than willing to share and support information on healthy food choices and physical activity.

Investing in Your Health and Wellbeing

It's important for us to remind ourselves that one of the best investments we can make is in the health and wellbeing of ourselves and family members. We may be watching our dollars a little closer and giving up a few things that we've come to enjoy, but continuing to support the benefits of daily physical activity and nutritious eating are investments that will pay big dividends for many years to come. The returns on your investment will be priceless. Your family bonds will be closer. The quality of family time will be enhanced. Family stress will be reduced. Communication between family members will increase. Everyone, including

caregivers, will become more active. Physical and emotional benefits will be positive. Mom and dad may experience and rediscover the fun play games they loved as children. Participating in physical activity doesn't have to cost a lot or anything and is something you can control, unlike some of your monetary investments. A little extra planning can lead to many economic and healthier food choices. The dollar cost for healthier food choices and physical activity doesn't have to be a barrier. There may be many things we are giving up, but let's not have one of them be less physical activity in the home or community or less healthy food choices. Investing in and supporting everyone's health and wellness now and into the future will result in many cost savings for everyone.

Consider making your weekly family social activity an active one. Active transportation through "people power" can enhance how you get around for business and pleasure. It's great for the pocket book, environment and everyone's own physical, social, mental and emotional wellbeing. If, as a family, you'd normally drive to get somewhere, stop, and think, do I, we, really need to drive? Is it really that far? Could we as individual family members or as a family walk or run instead or, cycle to the location if time or distance is a little too far for some to walk or run. Do a little planning around the places you usually drive to and perhaps there are a few you might be able to "people power" to. Gas cost savings, cleaner environment, hmmm!

As the evenings get darker, consider taking a moonlight or flashlight walk around the neighbourhood after your family supper. Make your walk into a scavenger hunt, clean up your neighbourhood, or pick up a pointy rock, a red leaf, pine cone or discarded paper. Experience a scavenger hunt with your flashlight. More and more walkable community packages, including walking routes and maps, are springing up in many communities. Try a different walk each week. Many towns and cities have organized walking tours of various heritage and historical sites of interest. It might be fun to try, and everyone would learn a little more about the community they live in. Do you think you could consider a new active family hobby or tradition? What about walking and bird watching, rock collecting or orienteering? I'll bet there are many more you and your children can think of to do.

It may be challenging to start along this daily journey of investing in your family's active and healthy future. With a little bit of planning, it will become a necessary part of everyone's lifestyle and will become a fact in the way we choose to live and inspire the lives of your children, family and friends.

Active Inclusion—Active Children with Asthma

Caregivers agree that most children with asthma should be able to lead normal active lives. With good asthma management, most children should be able to participate in any sport or exercise. Controlled exposure to sports and exercise should be encouraged. Research has shown that regular exercise activity can improve lung function in children with asthma and make it easier for them to tolerate their symptoms when they do flare up.

A child can participate in many activities when their asthma is controlled. Many professional athletes with asthma compete in most sports with proper asthma care. For children with asthma, slow warmups prior to activity and cool downs after activity are important. Take doctor prescribed inhaled reliever medication prior to exercise and ensure the medication is nearby in case of breathing challenges during the activity.

Duffle Bag
keep your family's workout essentials
with you and ready to go

Youth Gear
make sure your entire
family has the right apparel
and footwear for your
active lifestyle

Running Gear and
Accessories Checklist

Socks
choose a comfortable pair

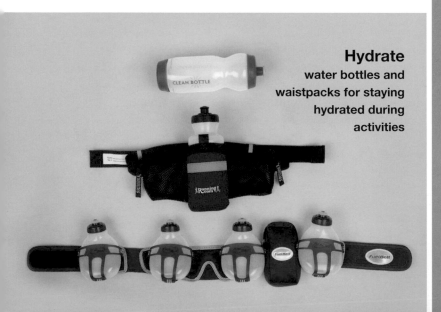

Hydrate
water bottles and
waistpacks for staying
hydrated during
activities

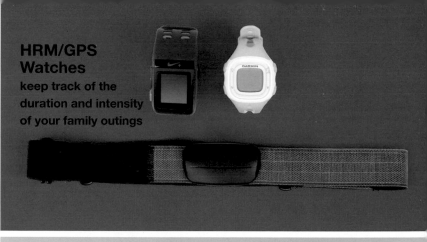

HRM/GPS Watches
keep track of the duration and intensity of your family outings

Adult Apparel
wear the right gear to keep up with your active kids

Stretching
gear to get you warmed-up

Sun and Skin Protection
keep yourself cool and protect your skin

FAQ

Common Questions and Answers

IS RUNNING GOOD FOR KIDS?

Absolutely, it's great for kids. It gets them outdoors, builds strong muscles, improves cardiovascular fitness, improves energy levels and helps maintain a health body weight. Are there risks? Yes, but Dr. Tim Noakes, professor of exercise and sports science, says, "It is important to stress, however, that there is no evidence for any negative physiological effects of intensive training by itself in the prepubertal period. There is no evidence that either children or adults can train themselves to the point where they suffer lasting physical impairment. ... Gifted young runners who chose to run 8K to 10K distances are at no greater risk of an unfavourable outcome or injury than adults completing the same distances under the same environmental conditions." In other words, be intelligent about the intensity and duration of young runners' training and consider their current level of fitness when encouraging them to run. But encourage them to run.

HOW SOON CAN KIDS START RUNNING?

Kids are natural runners; they run as part of play. They naturally run for fun and include rest breaks between short bursts of high-intensity running. If your child shows some interest in running at kindergarten age, he or she can run 100 to 400 metres. Having an organized start and finish line allows children to experience the world and culture of running. The key is to keep the programs informal, with little structure, and the focus on fun.

SHOULD I ENCOURAGE MY KIDS INTO TEAM SPORTS OR INDIVIDUAL SPORTS FOR SELF-DEVELOPMENT?

Both, and let them decide which is more fun and appealing to their individual personality. Team sports provide the physical aspects while also teaching kids teamwork, group motivation and organization. They will learn to get along with each other, the power of consensus and the acceptance of the coach's direction of the team. Individual sports allow kids to embrace and enjoy a sport they can practise and develop on their own. They also teach independence and self-reliance.

WHAT CAN I DO AS A PARENT TO HELP OUR FAMILY'S PHYSICAL ACTIVITY?

Be the best mentor and role model for your family by being active yourself. When kids see your daily activity, as natural as washing your hands, they will embrace exercise into their daily life. Also limit their screen time—far too much of our kids' time is spent here, which limits the time for fitness activities in their schedule.

CAN PHYSICAL ACTIVITY HELP OUR FAMILY BOND?

Sharing physical activities with your kids creates memories of times you spent having fun, laughing and enjoying each other's company. As a parent, you have the opportunity to forget the day's duties and spend one-on-one time with your child. From playing tag to flying a kit, having a

WHY DOES PHYSICAL ACTIVITY TEND TO DECLINE AS KIDS GET OLDER?

Like their adult family members, kids start to get busier with school and friends as they get older. Peer pressure increases and they can become discouraged if they are not keeping up to their friends. For many children, as they approach puberty they can feel ashamed of their own body image, which is an important driver to keep them active.

WHAT ARE SOME BENEFITS OF PHYSICAL ACTIVITY FOR PRE-TEENS AND TEENAGERS?

Besides the obvious fitness benefits, exercise reduces anxiety, stress and depression. We also know it improves self-esteem, enhances academic performance and provides a platform for a lifetime of healthy living.

family wrestling match or going for a hike you will get to share special moments and build memories and athletes for the future.

HOW DO I TEACH MY KIDS TO PLAY AND BE ACTIVE?

Kids are just like adults—they like power and mastery—so let them teach you some practised skill. They could give you a dance lesson, teach you their version of hopscotch or show you how to do the triple jump in the backyard. Families learn new skills when it is fun and social. Invite the neighbours to make it a community effort.

MY CHILD IS OVERWEIGHT. HOW DO I GET THEM MOVING AND ACTIVE?

Fitness is critical for the overweight child, but it is important to provide the right encouragement, so the child feels more confident about their body image and self esteem. Fun is always the magical factor. Let the child decide what activity is fun and non-threatening for them. Are they a potential rugby star or ballerina? Let them decide, and then provide the support and encouragement.

WHAT KIND OF REWARDS CAN I GIVE MY KIDS FOR PHYSICAL ACTIVITY?

Avoid ice cream, candy and soda pop. Instead, create a family challenge—family bragging rights are often the best reward. Plan a fun reward that everyone gets to enjoy as a family, thanks to celebrating the special achievement of the individual.

I WOULD LIKE TO GET MY FAMILY OUT FOR A WALK AFTER SUPPER 3 OR 4 TIMES PER WEEK, BUT THEY FIND IT BORING?

Call your walks a "search and celebration." Give everyone an object they must identify on the walk. In spring it could be the first visible flower in the neighbourhood; in winter, the longest icicle; on Valentine's Day, a rock in the shape of a heart; or in summer, the biggest leaf. Trust me, kids are natural competitors and maniacs about measurement. Who was first, who had a bigger cookie, who was faster—they love competition and it sparks family fun. There is nothing sweeter than beating a parent or a sibling in a game.

HOW SERIOUS OF AN ISSUE IS INACTIVITY WITH KIDS?

The heath effects of childhood obesity and inactivity is very serious. In North America it is at an epidemic level. Type 2 diabetes, hypertension, obstructive sleep apnea, fatty liver, poor self-esteem and a continuance into adult obesity, are just some of the concerns facing our families.

WHAT ARE SOME OF THE RISK FACTORS FOR INACTIVITY AND OBESITY IN CHILDREN?

The main factor is too much food, both in portion size and in calorie content, with many of the foods coming from high-fat, high-calorie groups, combined with processed junk food, juices and sodas. Lack of physical activity is another big factor. Lack of sleep and

family history are also contributors. Across North America, the rates of childhood obesity are approaching 20% of the population of children and adolescents. Clearly we all need to actively address the risk factors.

DO MY YOUNG CHILDREN NEED SPECIAL EQUIPMENT TO RUN AND BECOME ACTIVE?

To minimize the risk of injury, parents should have children wear proper footwear for many team and organized sports. Flip-flops, sandals and pull on shoes can be unsafe. Check with your coach to see what they recommend. The biggest concerns: be safe and have fun. A water bottle is a must have for all sports.

IS IT SAFE FOR KIDS TO PLAY OUTDOORS ON HOT DAYS?

Arrange for activities in shady areas or treed parks on hot days. In the backyard, a garden hose and sprinkler makes for pure summer fun. Also keep them drinking—water, not juice or soda.

You Can do it...Make Fitness a Family Affair

One of the most important gifts you can pass on to your family is a healthy lifestyle. Families that are physically fit are at a reduced risk of a variety of illness and disabilities. Families who exercise regularly have less feelings of depression and anxiety and feel a heightened sense of well-being. All of these benefits result from a small investment of your time: one hour per day or 4% of the day.

Make the most of your downtime. You set aside time for work and for other activities. Now is the time to set aside exercise time under the guise of family playtime. Instead of watching TV or playing around on your computer, go outside for a family walk. An evening walk can turn into a star-gazing adventure or flashlight fun walk with the kids. Split up the mentorship. One parent can be leading the adventure while the other cooks dinner. You could fly a kite, throw a Frisbee, jump rope or throw a ball; get everyone in the family involved. Keep in mind your children's ages. The younger the child, the more you must focus on play. As children grow older, they enjoy more competition and the thrill of winning against you. You win when you see how much their self-esteem and confidence improve. Together, you share in the physical activity and the laughter. Raking up a yard as a group or a garage cleanup can turn into a fun-filled family event with the addition of a stopwatch and some appointed teams. Keep music in your home and in your vehicles, because music encourages movement. A family "You think you can dance" contest can encourage fun and playful activity. Everyone gets to dance and to vote.

Pick a new activity to learn together. It could be dancing, lawn bowling, lawn darts, ladder golf, badminton or snowperson or sandcastle building. Engage everyone into the activity.

Keep a log of your progress: everyone needs a goal, a plan and a reward on completion. Rewards can be something as silly as an old recycled bowling trophy. Success of each individual needs to be celebrated by all of the family.

Family fitness does not require you to spend a lot of money on engaging physical activity. What it takes is motivation and a proactive approach that starts today, not tomorrow.

Throughout this book, we have provided some motivation, a great deal of information, some training guidance, nutritional guidelines and healthy food suggestions. In addition, there are two basic themes to the book: one, be a good mentor and active participant in your family's fitness; two, educate and lead your children in discussions about stress, nutrition, exercise and healthy body image.

Foster a team approach to all of the areas of family fitness so each one of them becomes a lifelong learning experience.

Families are unique. Cherish each family connection and adapt your goals to meet each one of them as individuals. Give your children the gift of family fitness. They will thank you for the rest of their lives. They, after all, are your heart and soul.

Biographies

John Stanton, Founder of The Running Room

John Stanton is a member of both the Canadian Retail Hall of Fame and Alberta Business Hall of Fame and author of eight books on running and one on walking. He is the recipient of the Dr. Harold N. Segall Award of Merit, which recognized his significant contribution to the prevention of cardiovascular disease and the promotion of cardiovascular health in Canadians. In 2010, the Canadian Medical Association awarded him the Award for Excellence in Health Promotion. He is Hon. Lt. Col. of the Loyal Edmonton Regiment. John is regularly featured on CBC, CTV and Global Television, in *the National Post, the Globe and Mail* and *the Vancouver Province* and on numerous radio and television programs across Canada and the United States. John Stanton is also a recipient of the Queen's Jubilee and Alberta Centennial Medals. He is a Member of the Order of Canada. He also received an honorary Doctor of Laws degree from the University of Alberta in 2012.

John has run over 60 marathons, hundreds of road races and numerous triathlons, including the Hawaiian World Championship Ironman competition. His pre-dawn runs would ultimately become John Stanton's 10:1 run/walk combination that has helped close to a million people do everything from learn to run to complete marathons.

The first Running Room store opened in 1984 in an 8x10 foot room of an old house shared with a hairdressing shop in Edmonton. More than 25 years later, the Running Room is one of North America's most recognized names in specialty retail. John's sons, John Jr. and Jason, are now partners with John in the family-owned company, with over 120 stores and 1,500 employees in Canada and the USA.

Don Zabloski, Family Fitness Consultant

Don has worked with Edmonton Public Schools for 33 years, 18 of those years as the K-12 Physical Education, Health and Athletics consultant providing advice and assistance to students, staff, parents and community members with their personal desires and choices for living an active and healthy lifestyle.

Don has demonstrated a career-long commitment to gender equity in physical education, sport and recreation through his philosophy and practice. He is an accomplished leader in the promotion of active and healthy lifestyles, both from personal and professional perspectives and as a skillful mentor, innovator and role model.

Don has co-authored many professional educational resources, including Alberta Educations' Physical Education and Health Curricula and Daily Physical Activity Guidelines; Safety Guidelines for Physical Activity; Safety Guidelines for Secondary School Athletics; and Edmonton Public Schools' K-6 ABCD's of Movement grade level resources.

For his contributions, Don has been recognized by Edmonton Public Schools' Board of Trustees–District Recognition Award; Alberta Teachers Association Health and Physical Education Council–Distinguished Service Award; and Alberta Schools' Athletic Association—Robert H. Routledge Award of Merit.

Don has been a Running Room team member for many years, teaching clinics, hosting numerous Running Room sponsored run/walk events and sharing his expertiese through the *Running Room Magazine's* Active Families articles.

This book presents the best of Active Families, as the Running Room continues to provide the necessary supports for families of all ages, with the knowledge, skills and attitudes necessary to live active and healthy lifestyles.

Online Resources

Running Room Sites

www.runningroom.com
www.events.runningroom.com
www.ca.shop.runningroom.com
www.us.shop.runningroom.com
www.runningroom.com/mobile
www.rapid-registration.com

Mobile Runner Pro and Pace
Calculator Free both available
on Google play and iTunes.

Community Sites

www.facebook.com/runningroominc
www.facebook.com/johnstantonrunningroom
www.twitter.com/RunningRoom
www.twitter.com/JohnStantonRR
www.pinterest.com/runningroom
Google+ Running Room
Google+ John Stanton

Other Resources

www.marjorieoconnor.com
www.caringforkids.cps.ca
www.activehealthykids.ca
www.hc-sc.gc.ca
www.eatwellbeactive.gc.ca
www.EATracker.ca
www.physiotherapy.ca
www.cma.ca
www.ccs.ca
www.participaction.com

All stock photos: www.sxc.hu

Index

This index lists pages where you will find descriptions of various concepts and terms in this book. (It is not meant to be a comprehensive list for every time a word appears.